The Giant Awakes

Jim Graham

Marshalls

To Anne, who by her love, patience and loyalty has constantly helped me to be a member of the body of Christ

Acknowledgments

I am grateful to God for making me aware that he wanted me to be a member of the body of Christ; to Gold Hill Baptist Church, Chalfont St Peter, which so patiently and lovingly has allowed me over these years described in this book to grow and develop with them as God revealed his word to us; particularly to those who meet each morning in the church building for prayer, who have included me in their prayers and encouraged me in the writing of the book; and finally to Miss Pam Kerr who so willingly typed and corrected the manuscript.

Marshalls Paperbacks
Marshall Morgan & Scott
1 Bath Street, London EC1V 9LB

Copyright © Jim Graham 1982

First published by Marshall Morgan & Scott 1982

ISBN 0 551 01009 6

Printed in Great Britain by Hunt Barnard Printing, Aylesbury

Contents

Introduction

In the last 100 years, on the evidence collected by the medical profession, the tallest man ever was Robert Peshing Wadlaw. Born on 22 February, 1918, in Alton, Illinois, USA, weighing 8½lbs. He died 22 years later on 15 July, 1940, in Manistee, Michigan, and reached the incredible height of 272cm (8ft 11.1ins). He makes a very favourable comparison with Goliath of Gath, who was six cubits and a span, i.e. 290cm (9ft 6½ins). Statistics like these can be interpreted by only one word – giants.

Another 'giant' lives and continues to grow in the world today. The Christian Church is the major religion of five of the eight areas into which the world can be divided (i.e. the Western World; Africa; Latin America; the Communist Bloc; Asia; the Pacific; the Caribbean; and the Middle East). Christians number 1,300 million. This is not a static situation since 63,000 Christians are being added to the Church every day, and 1,600 churches are being born every week.

A great deal has been said and written about the Church's lethargy and even deadness. The consequence is often depression, pessimism and despair. Over these past years I have constantly read articles and publications in which our inadequacies and ineptitudes are examined with ruthless frankness. Indeed, self-judgment – in a collective sense – is almost as fashionable in Christian circles as is self-congratulation in the political sphere.

Most of us are familiar with the picture drawn by Rita Snowden in *When We Two Walked* where she tells of a walking tour which she and a friend made in the South of England. One Sunday they came to a little village church and went in to worship. They found three in the choir, perhaps twenty in the congregation, and the vicar.

> Hymn and psalm and prayer, and the quiet murmuring voice of the Vicar tended to take my thoughts out of the windows into the morning sunlight and over the fields and far away. The pity is, it was all so harmless, so gentle, so proper. There was nothing to remind anyone of that Young Man, Who strode the countryside and talked with the country people of Galilee, in burning words. . . . The kind of Man Who leaves you restless ever afterwards until you have found His God, and learned to call Him 'Father' too.

Even though the details may vary, this is a very recognisable picture, the kind of worship and atmosphere where there is an indulgent formality and a drowsy peace which is more likely to send a man to sleep than galvanise him into action in a real world, answering real questions and solving real problems, because he himself has unquestionably touched reality.

What has been the consequence of all this self-examination, frank appraisal and devastating condemnation? Often cynicism and loss of faith. I am reminded of how Thomas Chalmers was once congratulated on a brilliant and relevant speech which he delivered in the General Assembly of the Church of Scotland. 'Yes' said Chalmers in response to his admirers, 'but what happened?' This must be the test of examination and analysis – does it heal having wounded? Does it build having destroyed?

This book is written from my heart as well as from my head, with a resounding and uncompromising conviction: 'I believe in the Church.' I see signs of unmistakeable life, reality and activity on other Continents than Europe – but surely on this Continent too the sleeping giant is stirring. This undoubtedly is a day of hope when God is touching the body of his Son on earth yet again with thrilling and marvellous consequences. I am sometimes almost overwhelmed by the reality of being involved, since I am writing from within the tension and pressure and opportunities of the pastorate.

The Christian Church has always been the target of bitter hostility. Writers like Celsus in the second century and Voltaire and Gibbon in the eighteenth century, have accused her not merely of intolerance but even of crimes against humanity. There was a day when antagonism was proclaimed by the brilliant few, but in the twentieth century the disregard of and the apathy towards the Church of the inarticulate masses has been even more devasting. Predictions about the decay and early dissolution of the Church are no new thing in history. Long ago, however, they were answered in the memorable words of Theodore Beza to King Henry of Navarre:

> Sire, it belongs in truth to the Church of God, in the Name of Whom I speak, to receive blows, and not to give them, but it will please your Majesty to remember that the Church is an anvil which has worn out many a hammer.

As with his servant, so our Lord's words throb with a similar conviction of the indestructible nature of the Church. At Caesarea Philippi on the way to the cross, Jesus, with a passionate intensity which is unmistakeable when we read these words, declares: 'And I tell you that you are Peter and on this rock I will build my Church and the gates of Hades will not overcome it' (Matt. 16:18).

At times the Church has been sick and the illness has seemed to be terminal; weakened not so much by attack from outside as by apostasy from within. On more than one occasion in history it looked as if God himself had abandoned her. Prior to the Reformation, when Popes vied with one another in political intrigue and moral lechery, the outlook was indeed grim. So it was in the sixteenth century when a monk by the name of Tetzel went about selling indulgencies at exorbitant prices. So it was in the eighteenth century when an English king complained that more than half of his bishops were atheists. Such has been the catalogue of sadness in history, and yet the Church not only

6

remains alive, but is growing faster today than at any other time in her history.

I suppose this book was born in 1955 when, as a student, I went one weekend to the Scottish town of Kirkcaldy in Fife to preach. I was given warm and generous hospitality there by a father and daughter, and on leaving they gave me a book called *The Young Church in Action*. The Translators Preface to this modern English translation of the Acts of the Apostles by J. B. Phillips planted a seed of longing and faith in my heart that I would live to see such realities in my lifetime. I believe I have touched the borders of these things.

In his preface J. B. Phillips writes:

It is impossible to spend several months in close study of the remarkable short book, conventionally known as the Acts of the Apostles, without being profoundly stirred and, to be honest, disturbed. The reader is stirred because he is seeing Christianity, the real thing, in action for the first time in human history. The new-born Church, as vulnerable as any human child, having neither money and influence nor power in the ordinary sense, is setting forth joyfully and courageously to win the pagan world for God through Christ. The young Church, like all young creatures, is appealing in its simplicity and single-heartedness. Here we are seeing the Church in its first youth, valiant and unspoiled – a body of ordinary men and women joined in an unconquerable fellowship never before seen on this earth.

Yet we cannot help feeling disturbed as well as moved, for this surely is the Church as it was meant to be. It is vigorous and flexible, for these are the days before it ever became fat and short of breath through prosperity, or muscle-bound by over-organisation. These men did not make 'acts of faith', they believed; they did not 'say their prayers', they really prayed. They did not hold conferences on psychosomatic medicine, they simply healed the sick. But if they were uncomplicated and naïve by modern standards we have ruefully to admit that they were open on the God-ward side in a way that is almost unknown today.

The following pages contain what I believe to be the means whereby 'the sleeping giant' will not only stir but arise with an awesome reality and confront and challenge the Kingdom of Darkness. The challenge of the task is before us and the pain and discomfort has to be faced. The call of my heart is not to novelty, but for flexibility under the wind of the Holy Spirit. The stirrings have begun.

John Newton once said of himself as an individual what the Church corporately might well say now towards the end of the twentieth century: 'I am not what I ought to be; I am not what I would like to be; I am not what I hope to be. But I am not what I was; and by the grace of God I am what I am.'

1: The giant needs a check-up

A few years ago the Elders of our church decided that I should go for a medical check-up. I have never really been quite sure whether it was my age, my appearance or my activity which sparked off such a decision! However, I went. For half-an-hour I was subjected to a thorough medical examination – pulse rate; blood pressure; reflexes; blood count; eye-sight; etc. At the end of it all, I had the satisfaction and alarm of hearing my doctor say: 'You are really quite fit for a man of your age' – the sting was in the tail! I suppose if I had compared myself with someone from a Third World country I would have been declared healthy without the palaver of a medical examination, but against the norm 'for a man of my age' I was medically acceptable.

The Church in every age is often in danger of being satisfied with itself because it compares itself with other churches. Even churches which are making a significant impact and showing themselves as particularly relevant are 'explained' because of their setting or the culture in which they live, either socially or nationally. Consequently, their 'success' does not impress us. We need to have a check-up against God's norm.

The English word 'church' is derived from the Greek adjective *kyriakos* as used in such phrases as *kyriakom dōma* or *kyriakē oikia*, meaning 'the Lord's house' i.e. a Christian place of worship. This can be so misleading, and has led to a deep-seated misunderstanding that the Church is a building. In most of our minds that concept is difficult to eradicate. So often we have a mental picture of a building when we say: 'I am going to the church'. 'Church', in the New Testament, however, is always people and is a translation of the Greek word *ekklēsia* which is made up of two Greek words *ek* (out of) and *klesia* (from the verb meaning 'to call') i.e. 'called out of'.

Ekklēsia also has a Hebrew background. In the Septuagint (the Greek translation of the Hebrew Scriptures) on over seventy occasions it translates the Hebrew word *qahal* which again comes from a root which means 'to summon'. It is regularly used for the 'assembly' or the 'congregation' of the people of Israel. In the Hebrew sense it means 'God's people called together by God in order to listen to and act for God'.

In a sense the word 'congregation' loses a certain amount of its essential meaning. A 'congregation' is a company of people 'who have come together'. There is an implication there that it is optional, and the initiative lies in those who comprise it – it is at the mercy, the choice, the desire, and the preference of those who come or do not come.

A *qahal* or an *ekklesia*, however, is a body of people 'who have been called together'. The two original words, Hebrew and Greek, put all the emphasis on the action of God. So the Church is not a body of people who come together because they have chosen to do so or even because they enjoy doing so, but they assemble because God has called them to himself. They come together not to hear or share their own thoughts or opinions, but to listen to the voice of God, so that having heard what he is saying to them they will respond in glad obedience.

This strikes right at the heart of our attitude towards the Church. We become part of it physically and actually not as an option, but as an obligation. The atmosphere is not that of the cinema where I am entertained, but of the court room where I am expected to be present; informed without question about the law of the land; and my response and reaction to what is said and done is immediate and is taken for granted.

So not only is the Church not a building, but neither is it an optional extra depending on the whim and fancy of the Christian. Rather, it is a gathering of people summoned by God to listen to him and to act upon his word. I sometimes ask myself: Is this the attitude and atmosphere of those with whom I gather together regularly? This is fundamental to any expression of the Church's life. Without it we cannot proceed. With it, who knows what will happen under the hand of God.

The concern of God is not so much to redeem individuals as to create a new community for himself. There is a phrase which occurs like a refrain through the Bible, 'I will be their God and they shall be my people.' It is significant that almost the final words of the Bible breathe this same yearning intention from the heart of God: 'And I heard a loud voice from the throne saying, "Now the dwelling of God is with men, and he will live with them. They will be his people, and God himself will be with them and be their God."' Long ago Lord Melbourne declared that 'religion is a private thing'. Unfortunately, he confused, as many of us have done, the words 'personal' and 'private'. Alan Stibbs once wrote, 'God made man for himself. The chief end of God in the creation of man was to have a people of whom he could say: I am theirs and they are mine. I will be their God, and they shall be my people. It is therefore God's unmistakable purpose to have a people of his own, and by his amazing grace it is the utterly undeserved privilege of all who belong to Christ to belong to this community, the people of God.'

Some years ago we were exploring Paul's letter to the Ephesians in our morning Bible School. All was going well until we came to Ephesians 4. There we got stuck for weeks on end. Generally, I have found that there are not too many problems when dealing with doctrine – and Ephesians 1–3 basically teaches doctrine. The problems begin to arise when you apply that doctrine in a practical way to life and so take it seriously. It came as a severe challenge to us that however much we ducked we could not get out of the way. Ephesians 4:1–16 became our check-up – our visit to the doctor for examination.

The Members of the Church (4:1–6)

We noticed, first of all, that this passage spoke very clearly about *the members of the Church*. We discovered that no matter how gifted, visionary, and competent the architect of a building might be; and no matter how able, conscientious and punctilious the builder might be; unless the right material was used, then the building would neither endure nor fulfil the function for which it was created. The key to the building lay in the material used in its construction. We noted that there are two ways in which 'being a member' could be understood. First, you can be a member of a club (e.g. a cricket club; a gardening club; a golf club) and so long as you pay your subscription (cf. offering); keep the rules (cf. acknowledge the Church Constitution); and show up with some regularity; you are regarded as a good club member. Secondly, membership can apply to the relationship of my arm or leg or foot to the rest of my body. If accidentally, surgically, or violently I lose a part of my body, I speak of it as being 'dismembered'.

The Church has been plagued by the first concept of membership – i.e. as others are interested in cricket or gardening or golf, so I am interested in Christianity, and as they join their club, so I join mine. Of course we would never dream of saying this, but in reality it is often true. Ian Thomas says:

If the way you live your life as a Christian can be explained in terms of *you*, what have you to offer to the man who lives next door. The way he lives his life can be explained in terms of *him*, and so far as he is concerned, you happen to be 'religious' – but he is not. 'Christianity' may be *your* hobby, but it is not *his*, and there is nothing about the way you practice it that strikes him as remarkable! There is nothing about you which leaves him guessing, and nothing commendable of which he does not feel himself equally capable without the inconvenience of becoming a Christian.

It is only when your quality of life *baffles* the neighbours that you are likely to *impress* them. It has got to become patently obvious to others that the kind of life you are living is not only *highly commendable*, but that it is beyond all *human explanation*. That it is beyond the consequences of man's capacity to *imitate* and, however little they may understand this clearly, the consequence only of God's capacity to *reproduce himself* in you.

The New Testament knows nothing of this 'club' kind of membership. It assumes and teaches 'body' membership – each living part must remain organically joined to the whole, otherwise it is irrelevant and without significance.

With this as a context, Paul spells out the characteristics of Church members based on all he has written in the first three chapters of his letter to the Ephesians. 'What the world needs to see is the wonder and beauty of God-possessed personalities; men and women with the life of God pulsating within them, who practise the presence of God and consequently make it easy for others to believe in God.' So wrote Duncan Campbell out of his experience of the Spirit of God moving in revival in the Western Islands of Scotland.

This will happen when Christians are 'completely humble' (v. 2). I discovered many years ago that other people can humiliate me, but there is only one person who can humble me. That person is me! Paul urges them – and us – to be 'completely gentle'. This is one of the lovely words of the New Testament. It means 'controlled strength': it could, for example, be used of a wild horse which has been captured and broken in, so that it is now responsive to the bit and the bridle. It has not lost any of its strength or personality, but that is now under control. An old teacher of mine described this characteristic as a man on the tiller of whose life was the hand of God.

It will be a life which manifests 'complete patience'. This always means patience with people rather than with things. Bishop Lightfoot has spoken of this as 'the spirit which refuses to retaliate'. What a beautiful – and supernatural – characteristic.

'Be completely . . . bearing with one another in love.' I

cannot find a better expression of this than that by Kenneth Taylor in the Living Bible when he paraphrases it as 'making allowances for other peoples faults'. It is the love which operates not in the area of my emotions and feelings, but in the area of my will and decisions.

'Make every effort to keep the unity of the Spirit. . .', and he goes on to develop this imperative in the next few verses. It is not a unity that we are to devise, but rather a unity we are to discover and then defend. It is not on the basis of natural attraction, but on the basis of supernatural activity. How little we really know of the fellowship of the Holy Spirit even when we know something of the grace of our Lord Jesus Christ and the love of God our Father.

At the time of writing, the absorbing question which continues to occupy us is: 'How do you ensure in a normal, local church situation that the Lord *has* the right material to build his Church?' It would be more profitable for us to spend time answering that question realistically than in answering most of the other questions which gain so much publicity on the Sunday Programme, the Religious Chat Shows, and the Christian periodicals, not to say anything of the Synods, Presbyteries, Councils and Church Meetings all over our land.

The Ministries of the Church (4:7–14)

We began to notice together that God never expects from us what he does not give to us – not because we have earned it, but out of the sheer undeserved generosity of his loving heart. God provides for us, not so that we shall become smug, selfish and self-satisfied, but so that we shall become relevant and effective. God has requirements which he expects to see met, and demands which he has the right to make upon us, but he provides in such lavish abundance that it is a liberating joy to become those who have been 'set free from sin and have become slaves to righteousness' (Rom. 6:18).

Unhappily, we have attempted to respond to God's demands from the Church without recognising God's provision for the Church. Where are the apostles, prophets, evangelists, pastors and the teachers in the Church today? Can you identify them clearly and with confidence? Without them it is clear that God's people will not be relevant in the world and his Church will be noticeably and undeniably impoverished, weak and immature.

The apostle is by derivation one who is sent out from the heart of the Church and recognised and supported by the Church to deliver God's word in such a way that people will receive it. He is an architect for the Church, indicating how it is to be built and develop. He is accountable to the Church for the ministry that he exercises.

The prophet has the difficult task, in these activist days, of waiting before God and listening to God in order to hear what the Lord is saying to his people. Then his task is so to declare that word uncompromisingly and with authority that the people of God will respond: 'This is from God for us in this hour.'

The evangelist is the spiritual midwife who has the joy, amid all the potentially complicated situations emerging, of bringing new spiritual children into the world. He has the responsibility of making sure that they are 'well born' and have a proper start in that spiritual life. All of us are called to be witnesses, but not all are called to be evangelists.

If the evangelist is the spiritual obstetrician, then the pastor or shepherd is the spiritual paediatrician. His task is to ensure that the new born child of God has the proper climate, food, rest, exercise and ecnouragement for the proper development and progress of his Christian life. His task will be negative as well as positive. He has the responsibility to say: 'You must not' as well as the responsibility to say: 'You must.'

The teacher's responsibility is perhaps the most self-evident. To change the picture somewhat – the soil in which a seed grows is fellowship; the climate in which it grows is the awareness of God; and the food by which it grows is the word of God. The teacher's task is so to expound and explain the word of God that it will be relevant and those who hear will be able to say: 'I understand that'; 'that really does make sense'.

The point of these ministries is 'to prepare God's people for works of service, so that the Body of Christ may be built up. . .' To 'prepare' or 'equip' is an interesting word – *ton katartismon*. It comes from a word which means 'to set' a broken limb or 'to put a joint back' which has been dislocated. In this sense it is a medical word which indicates that in its fulfilment often pain is caused from which the body shrinks. The same word is used for fishermen 'preparing' or 'mending' their nets which have been damaged and broken as they have fished (Mark 1:19). Whether it is used of people or things the implication is quite clear: these ministries are required to make sure that the people of God are functioning properly.

The real problem arises not only in identifying these ministries, but in implementing them in the functioning Body of Christ. The price of neglecting and disregarding them, however, is too high to contemplate. That bill has already come in for the Church in the West. We can never anticipate apostolic ends without utilising apostolic means. How hard we have tried to do God's work in our way. Why should we be surprised when we discover that it does not work?

The Maturity of the Church (4:15–16)

I remember visiting a family in Greenock on the banks of the River Clyde where there was obvious warmth and love – and yet heartbreak. There was only one daughter in the family and clearly she was loved by her parents. When I called she had just celebrated her thirty-second birthday. She had all the appearances of an adult in dress, hair-style, etc., but she was content to play with her dolls and live the make-believe life of a little child. While physically developed she remained immature and infantile mentally, emotionally and socially. It was not difficult to see the pain in the parents eyes, and to feel the hurt in their hearts.

The whole emphasis of the Bible is that God our Father wants his family to grow not only numerically, but in every other way. There is an aching yearning in this passage from the heart of God that we would grow up – become mature.

These two verses (4:15–16) are a grammarians nightmare! It is very difficult to tell where the main clause is, and what the subordinate clauses are. However, there are three main strands that can be quite easily unravelled and so understood. These three strands become God's characteristics for a mature Church.

1. Each member of the Church must be rightly related to the head of the Church – Jesus Christ

I remember visiting a patient in Stoke Mandeville hospital who had been involved in a car crash. I had never met him before, and when I was introduced to him as he lay on his bed, he seemed perfectly normal. His head and his body seemed to relate to each other. However, he did not respond to my outstretched hand – he could not. His neck was broken and he was paralysed from the neck downwards. There are other medical reasons which prevent the head relating properly to the body although all appears well at first sight. Yet it takes little intelligence to know that all is not well. I have noticed over the years that patients who suffer in this way have certain distinguishable characteristics

1. They are unable to move properly.
2. They are easily frustrated because they know what they want to do, but they are unable to do it.
3. They are very clumsy in achieving even the simplest tasks.
4. Normally they have difficulty in communicating, since their speech is either impaired or is non-existent.
5. They are easily tired-out, and unable to continue in the least demanding exercises.

If you raise all this to a spiritual level the parallels are strikingly apt. Often a church looks well related to the head – it holds its services, preaches its sermons, recites its creed, sings its hymns, says its prayers, continues its religious programme year in and year out. As it sits there in its building at the corner of the road all seems well – and yet clearly something is wrong because on a superficial examination it is not the Church as it is meant to be.

17

1. It does not move easily with confident authority and relevant activity to minister to a godless world.

2. It constantly displays frustration as it becomes aware of how it needs to act and re-act, but does not and cannot.

3. It seems to take forever to respond to and complete even the simplest tasks that a normal, ordinary household would have planned, accomplished and paid for as routine.

4. What it communicates to the world is often so tentative, uncertain and frankly contradictory, that no one really knows what it is saying or even if it is saying anything.

5. After any unusual exertion it is exhausted and protests the need to be given time to recover.

I do not want to overdraw the picture, but each of these things – or all of them – is a symptom of the body and the head not properly relating. The Bible makes it quite clear that the only cause of a breakdown in relationship between Christ and the members of his body, both collectively and individually, is sin. No amount of analysis, citing extenuating circumstances, pleading legitimate excuses, will let us disregard this spiritual reality – any breakdown between head and body is caused by sin. Sin is such an ugly, unattractive word. There are five main words for sin in the New Testament. It would be good to look at these so that we know what causes the breakdown between the head and the body resulting in such devastation.

1. *Hamartia* This is a shooting term and really means 'to miss the mark' i.e. I am not what I ought to be.

2. *Parabasis* This literally means 'to step across a line'. It has the idea within it of something which is deliberate, intentional, premeditated, and is in the area of my choice. It occurs when I find myself saying: 'I know I should not be doing this' – but I go ahead and do it; or 'I know I should not be saying this' – but I go ahead and say it.

3. *Paraptōma* This really means 'to slip across a line' and has the idea of something which is impulsive, unpremeditated, unintentional. It occurs when I find myself saying: 'I have no idea why I did that, it just happened' or 'I have no idea why I said that, it just seemed to slip out.'

4. *Anōmia* This means lawlessness. It embraces the

spirit which says: 'I will do what I want.' 'I will do what I think.' 'I will do what I feel.' It is the first attitude ever displayed by man in rebellion against God.

5. *Opheilēma* This means 'a debt' and indicates my failure to give to God and to man what is their due.

If the head and the body are going to be rightly related, then the problem which prevents this needs to be recognised and then repented of. Our great need in the Church is not only the power of the Holy Spirit, but pardon for what has come to be acceptable sin amongst us. We need not only to receive the Spirit, but to repent of sin. No health and vitality can be expected with sin unconfessed and undealt with. We need to call sin what God calls it – for God will only release us from the things which we call our enemies and not our friends – and then to confess it – for sin can only leave the body via the mouth. Only then will we know cleansing and healing and the head and the body will relate properly once more.

Some years ago a number of us from Gold Hill went away to share a church weekend. During the course of our Sunday afternoon Communion Service, quite unexpectedly, we began to know the reality of repentance. This was a new experience for us corporately and provided a milestone in our spiritual pilgrimage. However, it can never remain an historical experience to which we look back with thankfulness, but must be an ongoing experience. The question to be answered was: 'How can we live in such a fellowship together so as to ensure that not only corporately, but also individually, we are rightly related to the head?' That has demanded a fundamental reorganisation of our life together, which was a consequence of a fundamental re-appraisal of what the Lord required of us. We will look together at the practical implications of this later on.

2. *Each member must be in the place God has put him fulfilling the function God has given him*

The implications of the principle inherent in this characteristic were far-reaching. I held on to something which had been shared with me some years before, when I had become

19

aware of my personal need and went for help to someone who happened to be a missionary candidate at the WEC Missionary Headquarters nearby. During the evening, Peter said many things which have brought life to me through these past years. The particular truth which he gave me on that night that is relevant to what I am sharing here can be summed up in a little phrase: 'Revelation without experience leads to bondage' – i.e. if God shows us a spiritual reality, it is at our peril that we neglect or ignore it. I realised that many churches throughout the country with which I had some association were quite often (although not always) rich in revelation but woefully short in experiencing the reality of that revelation. The result has been spiritual paralysis. As a Fellowship we began to discover there were three very powerful things which could and would frustrate this principle.

First of all, ignorance. So many within the Church at heart feel they do not know where they are supposed to be nor do they know really what they are supposed to be doing. Of course, it is easy to hide from responsibility, commitment and involvement under the protection of ignorance. There can, in fact, be pain in finding out what we should know. For example, if I really discover the task God has for me in the Body of Christ it may affect my promotion prospects, my future security, my life-style, my pension scheme, my professional career, etc. It may shatter a few dreams that I have had – and that others have had for me. It may not – but, it may. Some time ago something akin to horror swept over my soul. It was the accompaniment of the thought: suppose I am busy and my life is taken up with things which God never intended me to do. These may not be bad or useless things but quite the reverse – good, acceptable, admirable, religious things – God's things. Better to face the pain of change now when there is still a bit of life left, than later when life is over and the bills have to be paid and an account has to be given to the Good Shepherd. After all he did say: 'You look after my things, and I will look after your things.'

The second thing which will frustrate the principle is

independence. The devil's strategy is isolation. He wants to put us and to keep us on our own. The strategy of Jesus, however, is fellowship. He wants to bring us into a significant, relevant and living relationship with the other members of his family. The whole concept of the Church as the Body of Christ reinforces this. Imagine, for example, the hand saying to the rest of the body: 'I am going to do what I want today apart from the body and regardless of it.' Actually, the hand is only relevant when it is not only attached to the body, but is co-ordinating with it. The principle is self-evident, but so difficult to grasp personally and practically.

The relevance and reality of my life as a Christian can only be seen in the light of my relationship to other Christians. The days when I could say: 'I will do what I think'; 'I will do what I want'; 'I will do what I feel' are gone forever. Some of us moved into Christian service and activity by making a unilateral declaration of spiritual independence. Some of us did not know any better, since no alternatives seemed to be available. But God has clearly declared and demonstrated that 'we become related to Christ singly, but we cannot live in Christ solitarily.' The days of evangelical individualism are over.

The third thing that I noticed which became a barrier to this second characteristic of a mature Church was a sense of inferiority. So many members of the Body of Christ feel their part is so small and trivial as not to matter. We began to learn as a church that many of us had been misled over the years over the nature of Christian vocation. This touched the very sensitive nerve of the problem. I was brought up to believe that you gave evidence of your Christian vocation by answering the question: 'What are you doing as a member of the Church?' The answer I was able to give was: 'I am a pastor.' Then we began to see that this was not the biblical principle. There were two quite different questions which needed to be asked and then answered by every Christian. First, 'Why are you doing what you are doing as a member of the Church?' There is only one satisfactory answer to that question: 'I am doing what I am doing because this is the claim God has on my life at this time.' Secondly, 'How are you doing what you are doing as a member of the Church?' There is only one satisfactory answer to that question too: 'I am doing what I am doing in the power and enabling of the Holy Spirit.' So we found that a sense of inferiority began to be dealt with as people replaced the *what* question with the *why* and the *how* questions.

3. Each member must be rightly related to the other members of the body

We will look more closely at this vital characteristic later on, but suffice it to say here that to claim to have a right relationship with God, if you like vertically, without knowing and having a right relationship with man, horizontally, is not only nonsense, but, in fact, deceitful. My relationship with God will be demonstrated in my relationship with man. If the latter is not viable, neither is the former. It is significant that in Genesis 3 man broke fellowship with God. As night follows day, Genesis 3 is followed by Genesis 4 and the biblical account of man breaking fellowship with man. Equally, when Jesus put man back into fellowship with God through his death on the cross, he also put man back into fellowship with man.

One last thing before we complete this 'check-up'. You will notice that Ephesians 4:15 begins with 'love' and Ephesians 4:16 ends with 'love'. This is the supernatural love of the cross made available and possible to us through the ministry of the Holy Spirit. In the human body the members may be co-ordinated properly and the joints rightly related, but all moving with considerable difficulty and pain. There is a physical problem caused when the lubricating fluid in the joints drains away. This fluid is called the synovial fluid – it enables the joints to move smoothly and painlessly. When this drains away it causes a condition which is familiar to many – arthritis. The love of God shed abroad in our hearts by the Holy Spirit is the synovial fluid of the body of Christ enabling the properly located, fully co-ordinated members to move easily and attractively in response to the direction of the head. What a glorious picture of health, vitality and effectiveness.

2: The diet for health and growth

On a lovely summer evening, twelve years after my ordination to the Christian ministry, I was leading our normal mid-week service, when I had an experience of God dealing with me which I find difficult to describe, but I would identify as my personal baptism in the Holy Spirit. In some ways it was unspectacular and undramatic, but in others it was revolutionary. The first impact of this experience was directly related to the Bible.

Ever since my ordination I had been convinced that nothing had been included in the Bible which was unnecessary, and nothing had been omitted from it which was necessary. However, I had been aware for some years that there had been a considerable gap between the biblical revelation and my experience as a Christian. Although uneasy about this, I had come to terms with the fact that this was 'normal Christianity'. Perhaps, pretentiously, I had come to assume that everyone was in a similar or comparable situation. In my more honest moments, however, it concerned me more than I admitted to myself. When I tried to cope with this situation I adopted two main tactics. One was to lower the biblical dimension by embracing a theological position which did just that. Although unsatisfactory, this was not too difficult to do – and was really quite comforting and reassuring. I found that in doing this I was in very good company. The other tactic was to increase my enthusiasm, devotion and commitment, which hopefully lifted me a little nearer to the biblical dimension. On that July evening, however, I think I saw clearly for the first time that God's provision for a man like me was to lift me in all my inadequacy into the biblical dimension by the power of his Holy Spirit. He was the one whom God had provided to enable me to begin to live the Jesus life now.

At that time I made another discovery which was to have significant effects upon my life and service. The Lord began to convict me about 'biblical hedge-hopping'. It was as if the Holy Spirit, who gave us the Bible, was unwilling to let me treat what he had given in such a dishonest and inconsistent way. What really alarmed me was that I was quite unaware of what I was doing. I would have defended my position and denied any such lack of integrity had anyone other than God challenged me about it. Let me illustrate what I mean by biblical 'hedge-hopping'. I had been happy to preach, expound and meditate in 1 Corinthians 11, but when I came to 1 Corinthians 12 there were a number of things which I did not fully understand and had no personal experience of, so I 'hopped' over 1 Corinthians 12 into 1 Corinthians 13 where I found myself revelling in that marvellous description of Calvary love. 1 Corinthians 13, incidentally, never asks us to do anything – it simply describes something. Whether that was a factor or not I cannot tell, but inevitably 1 Corinthians 13 gave way to 1 Corinthians 14 which is mainly about the dialogue between man and God in worship. I felt that this was a really strange chapter which did not quite fit my theological position, and again was outside my personal experience, so I gladly left it in favour of 1 Corinthians 15 which gives the most marvellous description of the resurrection body in the whole of Scripture. This is what I mean by biblical 'hedge-hopping'. The Lord made me very aware that it had to stop since it was quite unacceptable to him. It became clearer to me than it had ever been before that God does not reveal his heart and will to us to discover whether we like it or not. Nor does God reveal his truth to us for us to pass our opinion on it. God gives his word to us for one purpose only – so that we do it. God does not give us his word so that we can treat it like spiritual gourmets, selecting this and neglecting that,

25

enjoying this part and turning up our noses at that part. It is a diet that needs to be acknowledged and entered into by faith.

I remember being profoundly moved in the Coronation Service of Queen Elizabeth II, when the then Moderator of the General Assembly of the Church of Scotland, Dr Pitt-Watson, handed the Bible to the newly crowned Queen with the words, 'Here is wisdom. This is the Royal Law. These are the lively oracles of God.' In other words, this book is the law for monarchs. The Queen and her Parliament make the laws of Britain, but God makes laws for her. A law is not there for my approval, but for my action in recognition of it and in obedience and submission to it.

The influence of the Bible on our thoughts and speech is incalculable. The poetry of men like T. S. Eliot and Dylan Thomas is steeped in its idiom, and the verbal images of a dramatist like John Osbourne are strongly conditioned by it. But most impressive of all is the profound effect it has had on the hearts and lives of countless numbers of ordinary men and women. Martin Neimöller, kept in concentration camps for many years during World War II, had only one possession, a Bible. He wrote: 'The Bible: what did this book mean to me during the long and weary years of solitary confinement, and then for the last four years at Dachau Cell-Building? The Word of God was simply everything to me – comfort and strength, guidance and hope, master of my days and companion of my nights, the Bread which kept me from starvation, and the Water of Life which refreshed my soul. And even more: solitary confinement ceased to be solitary.'

Only for one year in modern history has the Bible not been the best-seller in Britain. That exceptional year was 1962, when D. H. Lawrence's *Lady Chatterley's Lover* – the subject of a notorious court case – went to the top. By 1963, however, the Bible was back on top and has stayed there ever since. This incredible library of sixty-six books, written in three different languages by forty different authors over a period of about 1500 years, with neither human editor nor organising committee, has only one theme: what

God wants us to be in Christ. The claims which are made for it are only surpassed by the claims which it makes for itself. It has only one ultimate author, the Holy Spirit. So its poetry, epic, prose, letters, proverbs (every literary form) combine to pursue this one great theme. It is a living book with a living author.

Until the close of the nineteenth century the Church had not been more united on any subject. The Greek word which expresses the source of the Bible (*theopneustos* or 'God-breathed') occurs only once in the Bible: 'All Scripture is God-breathed, and is useful for teaching, rebuking, correcting, and training in righteousness, so that the man of God may be thoroughly equipped for every good work' (2 Tim. 3:16–17). The term may well be defined as the divine 'in-breathing' into a man by God's controlling Spirit, with the result that he speaks or writes with a quality, insight, accuracy and authority which is possible in no other form of human speaking or writing. The exact description of how this occurred defies expression. I found it helpful to draw a parallel between the fusing of the human and the divine in producing the living Word and the fusing of the human and the divine in presenting the written word of God. The living Word – our Lord Jesus Christ – was brought into the world without the intervention of a human father. The Holy Spirit was the appointed agent. Mary, the mother of our Lord, remained a human mother, and her experiences throughout would appear to have been those of every other human mother – except that she was made astonishingly aware that her child was in fact to be the long-expected redeemer of Israel. She certainly brought other children into the world by the normal processes of birth. In the same way, the writers of the books of the Bible remained human authors, and their experiences appear to have been similarly natural, though, apparently, they were sometimes clearly aware that God was giving them a message of no ordinary importance. In the Old Testament on over 2,000 occasions the writers claim that God had spoken to them. For example, the prophet Ezekiel uses the phrase 'This is what the sovereign Lord says' or its equivalent, 200 times, and the phrase 'The word of the Lord came to me' 50 times. In the New Testament the apostle Paul says 'For I received from the Lord what I also passed on to you' (1 Cor. 11:23). The writers of the books of the Bible almost certainly wrote purely personal letters which were not necessarily of spiritual significance.

Someone has aptly said, 'The Bible is not an authorised collection of books, but a collection of authorised books.' Each of the books of the Bible passed three 'authority' tests before inclusion in the Scriptures.

1. The Author was Reputable

These books were, for the most part, written by men who were recognised as appointed by God to reveal his will – lawgivers and prophets in the Old Testament and the apostles and their immediate associates in the New Testament. This would not be an unusual test to apply to any writing – especially where it affects life quite fundamentally. I can remember receiving a letter some years ago which predicted my sudden and immediate death. While the first impact of reading it was devastating, on getting to the end, and reading the name of the person who had written it, I was somewhat reassured and relieved. She was quite unstable and an entirely unreliable person.

2. Agreement was always reached among the existing Churches about the intrinsic validity of each book

There was a quite extraordinary and surprising unanimity. Because of a lack of knowledge about their origin, a few books were temporarily doubted by a minority within the Church. This minority was at all times small, and there is no example of a book which was doubted by any large number of churches having been later accepted. The criterion which was decisive was that they looked for the embodiment of some part or aspect of the revelation of God or Christ.

3. *Their authority was recognisable*

The Books themselves clearly showed that they possessed the authority and inspiration of the Holy Spirit. In every case this was the final determining factor in deciding on its validity to be Scripture. Had this characteristic, so difficult to define and explain, been absent, then neither the authorship nor the agreement which had been reached would have compensated for it. It is very difficult to put into words what is meant by this internal evidence. Perhaps the best way to describe it is to compare Scripture with the Apocrypha – especially the New Testament Apocrypha. The external evidence of who wrote it and how their writings were received can only bring about a belief in their historical authenticity, whereas the Holy Spirit's witness brings a true spiritual persuasion of the reality of what the Bible claims to be – the word of God.

In 1540 Archbishop Thomas Cranmer said in his Preface to the epoch-making book the Great Bible, ordered to be set up for public reading in every church in the country:

> In the Scriptures be the fat pastures of the soul; therein is no venomous meat, no unwholesome thing; they be the very dainty and pure feeding. He that is ignorant shall find there what he should learn. . . Herein may princes learn how to govern their subjects; subjects obedience . . . to their princes; husbands how they should behave them unto their wives; how to educate their children: . . . and contrary the wives, children, and servants may know their duty to their husbands, parents and masters. Here may all manner of persons, men, women, young, old, learned, unlearned, rich, poor, priests, laymen, lords, ladies, officers, tenants, and mean men, virgins, wives, widows, lawyers, merchants, artificers, husbandmen and all manner of persons, of what estate or condition soever they be, may in this book learn all things what they ought to believe, what they ought to do, and what they should not do, as concerning Almighty God, as also concerning themselves and all others.

Slowly – very slowly – within our church we have been

29

walking in the direction that the Bible is the true reality and our experiences which are less than that dimension are not reality. We are discovering that many of us have lived for such a long time in abnormal (non-biblical) Christianity, that we have come to accept it as normal. When, at some point, we touch normal (biblical) Christianity it strikes us as being so unusual that we are prone to be critical and fearful and call it abnormal. Wherever the Sleeping Giant is stirring there is a grateful acceptance of the fact that 'God says it in his word; I believe it in my heart; and that settles it forever.'

In that greatest escape story of all time told so graphically in the Old Testament – the escape of more than two million of God's people from Egypt – God said to them after their emancipation, 'See, the Lord your God has given you the land. Go up and take possession of it as the Lord, the God of your fathers, told you. Do not be afraid; do not be discouraged' (Deut. 1:21). The response of God's people was to set up a committee which would carry out a survey of the land, which God had promised to give them and had told them to enter, in order to give a feasibility report. In other words, they were going to ascertain whether what God had told them to do could be done. There is an un-cannily familiar ring about that. The committee of twelve returned. Ten of them said: 'It cannot be done', only two said: 'It can be done.' They had been gripped by one of the deadliest diseases which had gripped the people of God in every generation – the paralysis of analysis. How often God has spoken and we have subjected the word of the Lord to our human reasoning and come to the conclusion it is not possible – and then found spiritual cliches to justify our unbelief, rebellion and disobedience. Mental analysis without the guidance of God results in hardness of heart. When we have a hard heart, we become hard of hearing spiritually. As far as God's people were concerned it took them forty years to find out that their way did not work. I frequently wonder how long it would take us to come to the conclusion that 'God says it in his word; . . . and that settles it' whether I believe it in my heart or not. God has called us to walk by faith and not by sight. Many of us have persuaded ourselves that we *are* walking by faith until we discover ourselves in unfamiliar, and sometimes hostile, circumstances, and then we begin to realise that, in fact, we are walking by sight.

Some years ago four principles emerged for me out of Deuteronomy 31:12 and 13: 'Assemble the people – men, women and children, and the aliens living in your towns – so that they can listen and learn to fear the Lord your God and follow carefully all the words of this law. Their children, who do not know this law, must hear it and learn to fear the Lord your God as long as you live in the land you are crossing the Jordan to possess.' These principles have become quite fundamental for me in any leadership that needs to be exercised with regard to the importance of the word of God in the local church. It meant a reorganis- ation of existing congregational patterns for our life together and a resistance of continuing attempts to remove these principles – often from the most unexpected people. Quite clearly this word is addressed to all God's people – not just the children, not just the adults, and not just the 'home' crowd. Any system of teaching the word of God must be completely comprehensive. The implications of this have been hard to maintain over the years. However, if you really believe that the divine imprimatur is upon what you are doing the difficulties are easier to face.

The first principle is to ensure that the people of God can *listen* to what God has to say to them. This seems so elementary, and yet is so fundamental. How can people enter in to what God has desired for them if they have not even heard what God has to say? Many live in spiritual poverty these days because their faith is built on a mixture of tradition, superstition, sentiment and prejudice.

The second principle follows from the first. It is not enough that God's people should *hear* his word; they must be *learning* from his word. Through the years it has become clear that while many *listen to* and *hear*, few are really *learning* the meaning and personal implication of what is being said. Our task is to ensure not only that people are hearing God's word, but that they are understanding and grasping its personal or corporate consequences. We need to answer *two questions* from those who have heard God's word. The first is: 'What does this mean?' The second is: 'What does this mean for me?' There are two Greek words in the New Testament which have considerable significance for us here – *rēma* and *logos*. Dr Karl Barth speaks of this difference as 'the word of God *to you*, which is *rēma*, and the word of God, *logos*, which is *universal*'. For example, the Bible, the Ten Commandments, the Gospels are all *logos* – the universal word of God to all men. Jesus Christ is the final *logos* to all men everywhere. He never changes, he is the same always. But before the *logos* can do us any good, it must become a *rēma*. For example, Romans 10:17 which is so often quoted among Christians says: 'Consequently, faith comes from hearing the message, and the message is heard through the word of Christ.' In Greek it is the *rēma* of Christ which is the word of God to *you*. Very few of us became Christians the first time we heard the Gospel. Perhaps, indeed, some heard the Gospel many times before repentance came and belief followed. Then there came the day when God spoke the word *to you* – it was clear, personal, significant, relevant, effective. In that moment the *logos* became a *rēma*.

Frequently in our Christian lives we become more and more aware that what God has said to us is not the word which God is speaking to someone else. For example, after a full and difficult day of ministry Jesus went off alone to pray, having instructed his disciples to go home across the Sea of Galilee. They had not gone very far when a storm arose, and no matter how hard they worked, nor how expertly they handled their boat, they had little control. In the middle of the night, what seemed to them like a ghost appeared. They were terror-stricken and panicked. Through the storm around them and the fear within them Jesus said: 'Take courage! It is I. Don't be afraid' (Matt. 14:22–33). With characteristic boldness Peter said: 'Lord, if it is you, tell me to come to you on the water.' Jesus replied quite simply: 'Come.' This, in fact, is the whole point of the story. Who was it who came to Jesus that night walking on the water? It was Peter. None of the other disciples got out of the boat to join him. They were content that Peter should go alone. When Jesus said: 'Come' it was a *rēma* for Peter and no one else. Over the years Christians have read this record and many have preached about it, but as far as I am aware no one has interpreted it as saying that the Scriptures teach that we do not need boats because we can now all walk on water. That would be an absurd conclusion because it was a *rēma* for Peter and no one else.

Similarly, in the incident involving Peter in John 21:18–22: Jesus is with his disciples after his resurrection and at last he has managed to get Peter to himself for the first time since Peter's denial. He says to Peter: 'I tell you the truth, when you were younger, you dressed yourself and went where you wanted; but when you are old you will stretch out your hands, and someone else will dress you and lead you where you do not want to go.' Jesus spoke in this way to warn Peter that one day he, too, would be crucified. He then quite simply says 'Follow Me.' Obviously disturbed by the word of the Lord, Peter asks Jesus about what lay ahead for his friend John. The reply he received was very much to the point and indicated that Jesus' *rēma* to Peter was not intended to be his *rēma* to John. We need to be sure not only of the meaning of the *logos*, but if, in fact, that *logos* has a *rēma*. What we are *listening* to and *learning* may be God's word (*logos*), but is it God's word (*rēma*) to me? We need to learn to distinguish between the *logos* which is universal, eternal, and objective, and the *rēma* which is particular, temporal and subjective.

Our concern within our Fellowship is to make sure that people are not only able to listen to the word of God, but also to grasp its meaning within its context, and how it affects them now and has a living significance for their lives. The teaching which is given on a Sunday morning in church is followed up on the following Tuesday evening in our House Fellowships under the careful leadership and guidance of our House Fellowship Leaders. To let people hear God's word without realistically ascertaining if they have grasped it and applied it is spiritually inexcusable and pastorally irresponsible.

The third principle is perhaps the most difficult of all for us. It is contained in the injunction in Deuteronomy to 'follow carefully all the words of this law'. Revelation without experience leads to bondage. To have God speak clearly – and particularly to speak clearly to us – without a faithful response of obedience has quite incalculable spiritual consequences. Our problem as Christians is often not one of ignorance, but of disobedience. Someone has well said: 'It is not the parts of the Bible which I do not understand which worry me, but the parts of the Bible which I do understand.' The third principle is closely connected with our concept of and response to the Lordship of Jesus Christ. 'Lord' (*kurios*) is the most commonly used title for Jesus. Paul uses it 212 times in his letters. For every occasion Jesus is called Saviour, he is called Lord 29 times. I receive a little booklet regularly from a church in the United States. I did not ask for it, nor do I subscribe to it, but nevertheless it comes. Often I discover some enriching things in it. I remember being arrested by the following, written by the pastor:

> We have made a great mistake in the Church trying to get people to accept Jesus as Saviour. That is unscriptural. Never once in the Bible does it talk about getting people to accept Jesus as Saviour. When we acknowledged him as Lord, at that point he becomes our Saviour. Today the Lord is trying to impress upon us again the radical nature of being a Christian. And what it means in essence is putting our lives under the Lordship of Jesus.

When Jesus set us free, he did not set us free to do what we like – that is real bondage. He set us free to do what he likes. We sometimes say to someone: 'Your wish is my command!' When a person becomes a Christian he looks into the face of God and says: 'Your command is my wish!' The word of God reveals to us what God wishes for us and from us.

The fourth principle is that having heard, understood, and obeyed, we can now with confidence pass it on and share it with those who are around us and will come after us. When truth is wedded to testimony we have a very persuasive message to share.

John Wesley declared the burning constraint of his heart:

I want to know one thing, the way to heaven. God Himself has condescended to teach me the way. He hath written it down in a book. O give me that book; at any price give me the book of God! I have it; here is knowledge enough for me. Let me be a man of one book. I sit down alone: only God is here. In His presence I open, I read His book; for this end to find the way to heaven. Does anything appear dark and intricate? I lift up my eyes to the Father of lights. I then search after and consider parallel passages. I meditate thereon. If any doubts still remain, I consult those who are experienced in the things of God: and then the writings whereby being dead they yet speak. And what I thus learn, that I teach.

That fire kept him in the saddle for fifty-three years travelling as many as 8,000 miles a year, during each of which he seldom preached less frequently than a thousand times. Augustine Birrell declares of John Wesley: 'You cannot cut him out of our national life . . . no man lived nearer the centre than John Wesley, neither Clive, nor Pitt, nor Johnson. No single figure influenced so many minds; no single voice touched so many hearts. No other man did such a life's work for England!' Lecky, the historian, says that the religious revolution begun in England by the preaching of the Wesleys is of greater historic importance than all the splendid victories by land and sea won under Pitt.

No wonder Luke uses 'the word' more than fifty times to describe the romantic historical record of the quite revolutionary impact which the Church had on the then known world after Pentecost. The book of Acts is an historical record of how the Church spread from Jerusalem – where the ratio of Christian to non-Christian on the day of Pentecost was one in 30,000 – to Rome in about thirty years. Here lies a fundamental key to the Church's relevance and authority. The Word and the Spirit came together in ordinary people. When that happens the consequence always and inevitably is supernatural and irrestible reality.

3: Worship – the giant flexes his muscles

Evelyn Underhill, in writing to the Conference of Church of England Clergy in 1928, said: 'We are drifting towards a religion which, consciously or unconsciously, keeps its eye on humanity rather than deity – a religion which lays all the stress on service and hardly any on awe.' It is all part of this man-centredness of Christianity which emphasises man and his need rather than God and his glory. Even worship can be trapped in this emphasis, so that it is controlled and curtailed by what is acceptable to and appeals to man (and this will be dominated by temperament, culture and tradition) and not by what is desired and appreciated by God. Many of the publications on 'praise' which have emerged during the past two decades have emphasised that praise will 'work' for you and do you good – and this is true. However, the purpose of praise is not so much to do man good as to do God good. The apostle Peter reminds us that the two priorities which are to be recognised by Christians as they come to God are worship and witness.

> As you come to him, the living stone – rejected by men, but chosen by God and precious to him – you also, like living stones, are being built into a spiritual house to be a holy priesthood, offering spiritual sacrifices acceptable to God through Jesus Christ . . . you are a chosen people, a royal priesthood, a holy nation, a people belonging to God, that you may declare the praises of him who called you out of darkness into his wonderful light (1 Pet. 2:4,5,9).

Our task and responsibility is to declare our praises of God to God first, before we proclaim him to man. Pentecost began in praise and then developed into preaching. Some of us have come from a church tradition which has prostituted the principle of the 'priesthood of all believers' to formulate and maintain a fleshly, non-biblical principle of democracy among God's people, when in fact that very principle is given to secure the direct devotion of all God's people. In other words, the priesthood of all believers is Godward not manward.

Through the years man has been aware of a deep difference between men and beasts. Similarities have been comparatively easy to recognise, but man quite objectively has been aware that comparison has also yielded significant differences. Men have said, for example, that man is the thinking animal, or that he is the laughing animal, or that he is the only animal with a conscience. The one mark, however, which forever distinguishes man from all other forms of life on earth is that he is a worshipper; he has a bent and a capacity for worship. Dr A. W. Tozer makes the point very convincingly:

> Apart from his position as a worshipper of God, man has no sure key to his own being; he is but a higher animal, being born much as any other animal, going through the cycle of his life here on earth and dying at last without knowing what the whole thing is about. If that is all for him, if he has no more reason than the beast for living, then it is an odd thing indeed that he is the only one of the animals that worries about himself, that wonders, that asks questions of the universe. The very fact that he does these things tells the wise man that somewhere there is one to whom he owes allegiance, one before whom he should kneel and do homage.

Often the times when we come together as Christians are characterised by good humour, affability, cameraderie, zeal, high spirits (all, in themselves, pleasant and commendable enough); hardly ever do we find gatherings which are unmistakeably characterised by the overshadowing of the presence of God. We seem, at our very best, to be content with correct doctrine, pleasing personalities, lively tunes, and religious amusements. If biblical Christianity is to survive the fundamental pressures that cause apparently limitless pressure both from within and from outside the Body of Christ, we shall need to recapture the spirit of worship. We shall need to have a fresh revelation of the greatness of God and the strength and beauty of Jesus. We shall need to abandon our fears and our prejudices against the deeper life, and seek again, with humility and expectation, to be filled with the Holy Spirit. He is the only one who can raise our cold hearts to rapture and restore again the lost art of true worship. Where the Sleeping Giant is stirring a new dimension of worship is being experienced and expressed.

I do not know of a better definition of worship anywhere than that given by the late Archbishop of Canterbury, William Temple: 'Worship is the submission of all our nature to God. It is the quickening of the conscience by his holiness; the nourishment of mind with his truth; the purifying of imagination by his beauty; the opening of the heart to his love; the surrender of will to his purpose – and all this is gathered up in adoration, the most selfless emotion of which our nature is capable.' In the light of this it would seem unnecessary to pursue the question of why worship has such a high priority for Christians. However, in preparing some teaching on worship, the following things emerged from the Bible.

1. Worship is the first and greatest commandment

Love the Lord your God with all your heart and with all your soul and with all your mind. This is the first and greatest commandment (Matt. 22:37).

This is a salutary reminder that our responsibility to our 'horizontal' relationships comes second only to this first.

2. Worship is the first thing we should do when we come into God's presence

Enter his gates with thanksgiving and his courts with praise; give thanks to him and praise his name (Ps. 100:4).

There is a heresy which persists, even in this century, that laughter is a breach of Christian good manners. There is a feeling lurking somewhere in the recesses of our mind that the highest expression of the Jesus life must be solemn and sombre. In the same way, there is a feeling that Christian etiquette in worship is breached by an expression of exuberance and natural joy. The psalmist here encourages high spirits of the soul as we come into the presence of God.

3. Worship is the first response we make when we come to Christ

As you come to him, the living stone – rejected by men, but chosen by God and precious to him – you also, like living stones, are being built into a spiritual house to be a holy priesthood, offering spiritual sacrifices acceptable to God through Jesus Christ (1 Pet. 2:4–5).

God wants us to know from the very beginning that we have not only been created *by* him, but we are created *for* him. Worship, in essence, is not really to do with organs, pianos, guitars and tambourines, or hymns, choruses, anthems and vespers, or raised hands, bent knees, closed eyes, and prostrate bodies; but with the purposes of God. That is why the world stereotypes it; the flesh recoils from it; and the devil hates it.

4. Worship is the first mark of the Holy Spirit within us

For you did not receive a spirit that makes you a slave again to fear, but you received the Spirit of sonship. And by him we cry, 'Abba, Father' (Rom. 8:15).

There are at least seven different words in the New Testament for worship. Six of these occur only once, but the seventh occurs sixty-six times – *proskuneō*. It means: 'To come toward to kiss'. As we allow the Holy Spirit to have his way in our hearts as well as in our minds, there is the quite devastating dawning of the reality that the God who created the whole universe, maintains all life and all living, holds the stars in their courses, controls the ebb and flow of the tide, never fails in securing summer and winter, springtime and harvest, is my Father. I have a warm, intimate, secure, loving relationship with God. That is an awesome thing.

5. *Worship is the first sign of the filling of the Holy Spirit*
Do not get drunk on wine, which leads to debauchery. Instead, be filled with the Spirit. Speak to one another with psalms, hymns and spiritual songs. Sing and make music in your heart to the Lord, always giving thanks to God the Father for everything, in the name of our Lord Jesus Christ. (Eph. 5:18–20).

There are three kinds of songs which the Christian can sing. The first comes from the Jewish Psalter. The Christian can quite legitimately and with profit sing them all. The second comes from the verse and prose composed by Christians often for Christians. The third is much more personal and is not composed by man, but is communicated by God. We have found in our Fellowship that when the Holy Spirit is allowed to flow freely amongst us he gives to one and another, not only words, but also music to enrich us. Significantly, the Spirit not only directs us to bless God in our worship, but 'to speak to one another' and so benefit and encourage one another in worship. Many of the hymns that are familiar and loved by us are addressed not to God, but to us. It is worth examining the hymnbook to see how this occurs. Two things characterise corporate worship – we come together to *bless* God and to *benefit* one another. My concern in worship is how can I enrich God? And how can I encourage others?

6. Worship is one of the first characteristics of the early Church

Every day they continued to meet together in the temple courts. They broke bread in their homes and ate together with glad and sincere hearts, praising God and enjoying the favour of all the people (Acts 2:46–7).

The New Testament is a book of joy. The verb 'to rejoice' (*chairein*) occurs seventy-two times in the New Testament and the noun 'joy' (*chara*) occurs sixty-six times. This was one of the most powerful features of the Church that originally impressed society. Charles Spurgeon wrote to his students: 'An individual who has no geniality about him had better be an undertaker and bury the dead, for he will never succeed in influencing the living.' Ecstatic joy has not always been the most impressive thing in a Western congregation.

7. Worship is the first essential to hearing God speaking to us

While they were worshipping the Lord and fasting, the Holy Spirit said, 'Set apart for me Barnabas and Saul for the work to which I have called them (Acts 13:2).

As a result of hearing God speak so clearly, and acting in obedience to what he said, the Church grew rapidly in Asia Minor. In fact Luke records the facts in a brief but convincing way: 'So the churches were strengthened in the faith and grew daily in numbers.' We need to look again at how we organise our affairs corporately so that we know the decisions we make before God are led by the Holy Spirit. In doing this worship cannot be reduced to a formality.

There is not a great deal of specific information in the Bible regarding the form which was adopted when the people of God came together. The synagogue service was created out of the fact that the Temple was destroyed and God's people were exiled in Babylon. It seemed to include the following:

1. The Shema (or Jewish Creed)
2. Prayers

3. Readings from the Scripture
4. Exposition

Jesus would be familiar with both the Temple and synagogue services, since he participated in both. It is almost certain that Christian worship was modelled on the synagogue service when the break with formal Judaism finally came. The New Testament is somewhat vague about corporate worship with regard to its detail. Clearly the main day of worship was the Lord's Day. 'On the first day of the week we came together to break bread.' This obviously had certain practical implications for Christians since the first day of the week was a normal working day for the first 300 years of the Christian Church. Significantly, it did not hinder the Church from growing rapidly during these first few centuries.

The trap of confusing the Church with a building was avoided by the early Christians since they met in believers' homes. The key-note to the whole proceedings was simplicity. The ingredients were:

1. Praise

This seems to have been quite different from the rather restrained and formal practice to which many in the Western world are accustomed. For example, the Old Testament uses three main words in this context.

a. *halal* – the root meaning of this word literally means 'to make a noise'.
b. *yada* – originally this word was associated with bodily actions and gestures which accompanied praising God.
c. *zamar* – interestingly this word was associated with the playing or the singing of music.

The favourite word in the New Testament is *eucharistein* (literally 'to give thanks'). From this word we get our word 'Eucharist'. This is a much warmer and more intimate word than *eulogein* (literally 'to bless') from which we get our word 'eulogy'.

43

2. Prayer

The prayers of the Christian congregation appear to have been set as well as being spontaneous. Of the twenty-eight chapters of the Acts of the Apostles, twenty either refer to or give an account of prayer. Prayer was the inter-continental ballistic missile of the Church in that it could reach any point on earth; hit the target without fail; was equipped with a delayed detonation mechanism; had no defence against it; travelled at the speed of thought; and was fuelled by faith. Jesus had taught his disciples to pray in two ways. First, they were to pray out to the limits: 'ask me for anything'; 'whatever you ask for . . . I will do'. Incredible limits. But secondly, Jesus instructed his followers to pray within limits. They were to pray for 'God's glory' and 'in Jesus' name'. Our difficulties in prayer often are caused by our uncertainty and confusion that what we are asking will show God's essential being, fulness and brightness. In other words if God should answer this prayer will it bring glory to him? Equally, praying 'in Jesus' name' was certainly not the addition of a little formula at the end of what was said to God, but rather saying with humility and certainty 'Father, this is Jesus calling'. So often we struggle in prayer because we know we have attitudes, motives, desires and ambitions which Jesus would not recognise. God in prayer is giving us a cheque-book for the bank of heaven which is crossed with two lines. One, for God's glory, and two, in Jesus' name. Given that crossed cheque you can sign it for whatever.

3. Reading and expounding the Scriptures

Bernard Miles uses an interesting title for his Chilternian translation of some of the gospel stories – 'God's Brain-wave'. The early Church obviously had caught hold of the Scriptures as God always taking the initiative and unveiling his solution to man's problems and declaring his answers to man's questions.

4. A love feast which was followed by the Lord's supper
It is significant how much of the teaching of Jesus was given in the context of a meal. A meal is not only about eating, it is about relating. These early Christians were not familiar with instant food which was put into and retrieved from a micro-wave oven within minutes, served on plastic plates, and eaten on a stool facing the wall. A meal for them spoke of caring, loving, understanding and relating. Something happens, not only physically, but socially, emotionally and spiritually when Christians take the time and the trouble to sit down and eat a meal together. This is why Paul speaks so sternly to the Christian church at Corinth for their behaviour at the meal-time and their eating habits. The whole Jewish year seemed to revolve around meals. Jesus is found so often at a meal with people that he is accused of being a 'glutton and a drunkard'. So much of his teaching, ministry and miracles happened at a meal-table – not in a meeting with people sitting in rows on hard pews.

Within our Fellowship the Lord gave us five guiding principles for worship:

1. Our worship would be entirely glorifying to God.
2. Our worship would be that which expresses the essential unity of the Body of Christ.
3. Our worship would be that which maintains order and discipline yet does not limit freedom in the Spirit.
4. Our worship would give opportunity for the expression of varied gifts – both natural and spiritual – which exist among the people comprising the Body of Christ.
5. Our worship would help the Fellowship to come to the point of faith where the Holy Spirit can effectively work among us.

We noticed that the fullest evidence of what took place when the Church actually came together is in 1 Corinthians 11–14. Some of the characteristics of worship which emerged in 1 Corinthians 14 had profound practical implications.

1. Worship is to be expressed Audibly (v. 26)

'When you come together, everyone has a hymn, or a word of instruction, a revelation, a tongue or an interpretation. All of these must be done for the strengthening of the Church.' It presupposes that worshippers will come together, not with an attitude of what will I get from this exercise, but what will I be able to give. The whole chapter emphasises the dialogue of worship between God and man – God to man in prophecy; man to God in tongues. The instruction here is not: 'When you come together bring a holy silence with you.' Many are fully convinced that silence is public worship. Silence, clearly, is the exception rather than the rule. Silence can be pursued much better in private than in public.

2. Worship is to Make Sense (v. 6–13)

Everything which occurs is to be understood by the majority of people who are present. The main concern is not that all the worshippers will agree with what is being said and done, but that they will understand it. In fact, to be present at an experience of corporate worship without understanding what is going on is a waste of time.

3. Worship is to be in a Right Balance (v. 14–30)

Our experience of worship has been out of balance for so long that when balance comes to be restored by the Holy Spirit we say that true balance is out of balance. The mind will be employed in worship, but so also will the spirit – each will complement the other and enrich those who are participating. There will be preaching and teaching from the word of God, but also prophesying directly in the Spirit from God. As we have noticed, there will be hymns produced by godly men and women for Christians, but there will also be spiritual songs provided by God in the Spirit. There will be the response of the whole being (including the body) in worship and not just the intellect and the mouth. One aspect will not dominate the others.

4. *Worship will have an Order and Discipline about it* (*v. 27–33,40*)

Some can give an impression that unstructured, impromptu, vague, extempore worship is much more spiritual and acceptable to the Lord than worship which is prepared and disciplined and controlled. There is an order which is formal and dead – after all, the most orderly place in any community is the cemetery. But the order to which the Bible calls us is not that of the cemetery, but of the army. Liberty is not to be mistaken for licence. There will be freedom within the form; and spontaneity within the structure. God is a God of order and not confusion.

5. *Worship is to be Shared and not just Observed* (*v. 26*)

One of the characteristics of the Church is that people normally go for the back seats. As the Holy Spirit has been poured out on God's people, one of the areas fundamentally affected has been both private and corporate worship – and one of the evidences of this is that whilst in the past people have preferred the back to the front seats now the reverse is true! Worshippers want to be participants not spectators. This is an ecclesiastical revolution! People will come prepared to share what God has given, not as a result of intellectual ability, but because of spiritual awareness and communication. Often, over the years, we have depended on natural ability dedicated to God. This has led to the Church becoming middle-class and middle-aged. Now, however, as a new awareness of spiritual gifts as well as natural gifts has come, even the least likely, emotionally and temperamentally, are prepared to bring enrichment to the Body of Christ. The directive given here is that as many as can meaningfully and spiritually take part should do so.

6. *Worship is to have a Reality about it* (*v. 25*)

This cannot be organised, planned, or engineered. It is either present or absent – the sense and awareness that God is in this place and among these people. We come together in the first instance not to appreciate one another, but to be aware of God. The note of awesomeness is evident amidst all the imperfections and blemishes of the early Church. This will always be the criterion of relevance in the Church – 'God is really among you.'

We noticed two complementary principles at the end of 1 Corinthians 14. 'Therefore, my brothers, be eager to prophesy, and do not forbid speaking in tongues. But everything should be done in a fitting and orderly way.' The first concern is with those who would tend to exercise too much restraint, and the second concern is with those who would exercise too little restraint. God wants us to go as far as love will allow, and to keep going until love sets our limit. To take these characteristics seriously and to apply them practically has had a profound and dramatic effect on our attitude to worship and our expression of it. But then the Bible was never intended to provide motives for debate, but rather precepts for obedience, no matter how deeply this affects our traditions and our prejudices.

I was preparing to lead our evening Communion Service – a service which is perhaps the most relaxed in the month since the activity of Sunday is over and the responsibilities of Monday are not yet upon us – when I was arrested by a very familiar record in the Bible. It was the occasion on Jesus' last night outside Jerusalem prior to his crucifixion. He was not only out of sight of the city, but also out of reach of the Temple Guard. The crowds were already beginning to assemble for the celebration of the Passover; and more than two million Jews were expected as usual. Every male within a radius of fifteen miles of Jerusalem was obligated to attend, and there were many others besides from much further away. This was the largest gathering throughout the then known world. For one month in school and synagogue the Passover had been taught and highlighted. National feelings ran high since the Passover celebrated the supernatural intervention of God in delivering his people from slavery in Egypt. Could it possibly happen again that God would take the initiative and supernaturally intervene on his people's behalf – this time to secure deliverance from Rome? There was a kind of Spring fever in the air. Against this background of political intrigue, social injustice, national pride, and racial prejudice the very moving and comparatively private incident occurs of the woman anointing Jesus at Bethany. When we share Communion we can never be nearer to a more realistic time of worship. It burst in upon me like a sudden glory that here are key attitudes and activities which should characterise all our worship. Firstly, worship is a costly act beyond reason in its extravagance. The alabaster jar of very expensive perfume came from a rare plant in far-off India. In today's prices it would cost somewhere in the region of £7,500 for the half litre it contained. Normal hospitality would have offered a foot wash and perhaps the anointing of the guest with a few drops of relatively inexpensive perfume – just to freshen up. But perhaps the monetary value of the perfume was the smallest part of the price. That perfume had been bought and stored for one of two purposes – either to be offered as a dowry for marriage or to anoint her body for burial. In her response and worship to Jesus, the woman was surrendering her personal plans, ambitions and aspirations for the future and her social acceptability in the present. She broke the jar and so made it irreparable. I got to asking the question: 'Why did she do this?' I found two answers.

She did this because she recognised who Jesus really was – the unique, incarnate Son of God. Eastern custom directs that if a vessel is used to serve a very distinguished guest it is then destroyed in order that it may never be used to serve anyone of lesser importance. In the second place, she did this because she obviously knew what Jesus was going to do – not only would he die, but he would also rise from the dead. There would not be time to anoint his body in death in view of the time schedule of resurrection. The whole foundation of worship lies here – that we would recognise who Jesus really is and then acknowledge what he has accomplished so gloriously. True worship will always cost us the abandonment of our self-centred plans and ambitions. How we express this realistically will vary, but the reality will never be absent.

Secondly, and curiously an accompaniment of what has gone before, realistic worship will always evoke criticism.

49

There is more criticism over worship than over any other single activity in man's relationship with God. Significantly, the first recorded quarrel that man has with man is over a problem on worship (Gen. 4). Many still feel that it is a 'waste' to pour out anything directly on the Lord without having an end product in view. It sounds plausible and even spiritual to be concerned about the poor as a priority over worship. Without doubt social concern is commendable – Jesus required it; the world desperately needs it; but there is a place, a time, and a way to minister in abundant extravagance to the Lord so that we know that he knows our heart.

Thirdly, I realised that true worship requires brokenness. The alabaster jar permanently sealed in the precious nard perfume. The woman could have had it gift-wrapped with ribbons and given it to him as a gift. That, then, would have been an offering rather than worship. But in order to release its fragrance and make it effective, the jar had to be broken. So with us – worship is resident in the spirit of every true believer, but it is sealed up by the body and the soul (mind, emotion and will). Unless and until something happens to fracture the container, worship can never be released. In the life of our church we organise our programme so that as many as possible can go away to spend a week-end together once a year. This has been the pattern of our life together over many years. We were away for our second church week-end some years ago, and on the Sunday afternoon we gathered in a lovely drawing-room-like setting among the Kent hills to share Communion together. In those days there was a certain formality and even rigidity about this kind of event for us. However, prior to sharing the bread and wine, someone began to lead us in the song: 'Spirit of the Living God, fall afresh on me. Break me; melt me; mould me; fill me. Spirit of the Living God, fall afresh on me.' To our astonishment he did! There were gentle tears; tender confessions; God-honouring repentances; deep expressions of gratitude. To describe it is almost to destroy it, and certainly to misrepresent it. It was not humanly engineered, dramatic, intense emotionalism – but rather like the gentle rain of the Spirit of God falling upon our assembled dry and contrite hearts. There was a rightness; a beauty; a sensitivity about it all which defies human communication. The years that have followed have been characterised by a spiritual ebb and flow amongst us – but we have never ebbed beyond that point again. The human containers were fractured – as we had asked – and the oil of joy and worship was allowed to flow as an anointing upon the Body of our Lord.

The psalmist David speaks about this experience of brokenness in his own awakening to the reality of who God is and what God does. He declares with deep insight: 'The sacrifices of God (or "My sacrifice, O God, is. . .") are a broken spirit; a broken and contrite heart, O God, you will not despise.' 'A broken spirit'; is the translation of the Hebrew word *shabor* which means 'to shiver'; 'to break to pieces'; 'to reduce to splinters'. It is a spirit in that condition that God is looking for. 'A broken . . . heart' is the translation of the Hebrew work *dakah* which means 'to crumble'; 'to beat to pieces'; 'to bruise'; 'to crush'. It is a heart in that condition God is looking for. All true worship requires the splintering of our pride; the crumbling of our natural reserves; the bruising of our self-sufficiency; and the crushing of our self-will. Maybe it will be accompanied by tears of love, repentance, and submisssion. The hard-hearted can never worship God. They must forever be content with ritual and not reality. It is only the tender-hearted and the gentle-spirited who can pour out their inner spirit as an anointing upon God. All the encouragement we could ever need is expressed in Jesus' response to this act: 'She has done a beautiful thing to me.' In our worship, who is it that we are aiming to please?

Fourthly, as she broke the jar, she inevitably bore the fragrance of its contents herself. Some of it must have been retained on her hands and perhaps even on her hair. Because of the kind of perfume it was, for a long time she must have smelt like Jesus. Perhaps this is what Paul means when he says: 'But thanks be to God, who . . . through us spreads everywhere the fragrance of the knowledge of him.

We are to God the aroma of Christ among those who are being saved and those who are perishing.' True worship will not only affect God, but it will affect us and others to whom we go. This is what happened on the day of Pentecost – there was the 'smell' of the divine about the disciples of Christ as they worshipped God. Many remained to ask how and why it should be so. Peter, speaking on behalf of the others, told them. And so, that day, 3,000 were born into the Kingdom of God and began to live the Jesus life in the power of the Holy Spirit.

4: The Holy Spirit – life begins to flow

In 1963 two books were published and gained wide publicity. One marked the end of an era, the other signified the beginning of a new era. The former was entitled *Honest to God* by John Robinson; the latter *The Cross and the Switchblade* by David Wilkerson. David L. Edwards writing in that same year, comments in his book *The Honest to God Debate*:

> We all know that England is substantially a secular country. Their unpopularity might not matter, and might actually redound to their credit – if the churches possessed an inner confidence. It might then be suggested that people are offended by the churches' stern integrity, as people were offended by Jesus Christ himself. But as it is, we all know that, for the devoted labour to be observed in them, the English churches need a revival. They are not aflame with faith or overflowing with purposeful activity. They offend England not because they are too lively, but because most of them seem to have been decaying over the last half-century. This is why the stage is set in our time for a new Christian movement, to renew an ageing ecclesiastical tradition.

David Edwards looked to such men as John Robinson to be the catalyst for such a renewal. He looked to what some call 'religionless Christianity' to supply the answer to the cry of the Christian heart. He saw it, as others did, as a new deal for the enlightened humanist. He wanted a re-moulding of traditional Christian theology to suit the new age. In the event we discovered that God is much more concerned about renewal than man is. However deep man's dissatisfaction with 'religion' may be, God's is even deeper. What happened – and continues to happen – through the world was a re-assertion of the truth of the old theology and morality, but brought back to throbbing, relevant life by the power of the Holy Spirit. What God has done – and continues to do – is to assert again that the old Christian dogmas are true, but have become inert through the unbelief and lack of experience of those who declare them and hold them dear. He has challenged a position which complacently feels that it is right, but unfortunately it has become dead right. 'In the twentieth-century Christianity' writes Dr Carl Henry, 'the Holy Spirit is still a displaced person. . . Whenever the Church makes the Spirit of God a refugee, the Church, not the Spirit, becomes a vagabond.' Much earlier D. L. Moody, who was such a staunch expositor of what he unashamedly called 'the Baptism in the Spirit', referred to the day of Pentecost in this way:

> Now I believe the gift of the Holy Ghost that is spoken of is a gift for certain, but one that we have mislaid, overlooked and forgotten to seek for. If a man is only converted and we get him into the Church, we think the work is done – and we let him go right off to sleep – instead of urging him to seek the gift of the Holy Ghost that he may be anointed for the work. . . The world would soon be converted if all such were baptised with the Holy Ghost.

Over these years there has been a new appreciation of what Christians call the Gospel. In that, there has come a new awareness of what I like to call the 'salvation package'. I reflect with sadness that I received, and so consequently I declared for many years, an incomplete Gospel of salvation. What is considered biblically minimal and basic is that man must come to the place where he realises that in the sight of God (no matter how he feels, or how others regard him) he is a sinner. In the mercy of God he recognises that God loves him and knows his need even before he realised it himself, and taking the initiative God has provided his answer to this need – our Lord and Saviour Jesus Christ. Man requires and can enter into a living, personal relationship with Jesus Christ through repentance and accepting Jesus, the Son of God, as Lord and Saviour of his life. At the moment he does this in humility and faith the miracle of spiritual re-birth occurs. But the 'salvation package' contains much more than that. The New Testament indicates that he needs to be baptised in water in order that he might declare the old life to be dead and buried, and his new resurrection life to be given. He needs to be baptised in the Holy Spirit in order that he might be credited with the risen life of the Lord Jesus Christ. And to complete his initiation into the purposes of God he needs to become a living member of the Church of the living God, since we become related to Christ singly, but we cannot live in Christ solitarily. There is no such thing as a solitary Christian. Some of us spread these dynamic factors out over a long number of years through ignorance. We are grateful to God for his patience that waits to give us what he wants us to have right from the very beginning. The reality, however, lies not in a theological concept that we need to defend, but in a living experience that we need to display.

Dr Martyn Lloyd Jones, in the midst of his unique and effective ministry in the centre of London, declared:

> There is nothing, I am convinced, that so quenches the Spirit as the teaching which identifies the baptism of the Holy Ghost with regeneration. But it is a very commonly held teaching today, indeed it has been the popular view for many years. They say that the Baptism of the Holy Spirit is 'non-experimental', that it happens to everybody at regeneration. So we say, 'Ah well, I am already baptised with the Spirit, it happened when I was born again, it happened at my conversion; there is nothing for me to seek, I have got it all.' Got it all? Well, if you have got it all, I simply ask, in the name of God, why are you as you are? If you have got it all, why are you so unlike

New Testament Christians? Got it all! Got it all at your conversion! Well, where is it, I ask?

What we are concentrating on here is not spiritual birth, but spiritual baptism. As a young assistant minister in Glasgow, having fulfilled my responsibilities on a Sunday morning, I found that I could sneak off from time to time on a Sunday evening without ever being missed. Occasionally, I slipped in to the crowded evening congregation of St Georges Tron Church, in the heart of Glasgow, where the Rev Tom Allan was exercising the kind of profound ministry that made Glasgow confer on him the St Mungo Prize (awarded to the citizen who had contributed most to the city's life during the year). Tom Allan will never know the influence he had on my life in these years. He, along with my old Professor of Divinity at Trinity College, Glasgow, Dr J. G. Riddell, almost persuaded me to become a Presbyterian. God had called me to the ministry, and I longed with all the passion of a young man's heart to be really effective and not to succumb to a dull, conforming mediocrity. Tom Allan said: 'I have never been more convinced of the pressing need of those of us in the historic churches to be touched with the same fire that burns in Pentecostalism. Only a revived Church can bring revival to a lost and dying world.' My mind acquiesced; my heart yearned; but it was to be many years later before I knew the touch of that 'fire' in my own life. The Sleeping Giant is stirring in response to the reality of Pentecost within it.

There has been a great awareness of the impotence of the Church – particularly in the West. Many have felt that there must be more to Christianity than most of us have experienced. The challenge of the burgeoning Church, which is growing more rapidly today than at any other time in her history, has refused to be satisfied by turning a blind eye to its growth or by giving a proud, simplistic explanation for it. Many of us, too, have been aware of spiritual poverty in our personal lives, recognising that the Gospel proclaims not only forgiveness for sin, but freedom to live a righteous, godly life.

At the same time, as never before there has been the consciousness of the reality and pressure of the powers of darkness. Frank Smyth in *Modern Witchcraft* observes: 'Despite the fact that superstition has always been with us, the last few years of the 1960's saw a flowering of interest in occult matters which would have been inexplicable to an earlier generation. . . Now . . . it seems scarcely possible to pick up a newspaper or turn on a television set without some reference being made to ghosts, demons, magicians, or witches. The occult, which lay dormant for so many years, is once again up and thriving all around us.' These things have created a vacuum which the Holy Spirit came to fill. God never frustrates the longing of the heart for his glory.

The fundamental problem which confronts us as we think of the Holy Spirit is really grasping that he is a person. The problem is accentuated grammatically in that the Greek word for 'Spirit' is *pneuma* – and this is a neuter noun. In some older translations of the Bible *pneuma* is referred to as 'it' rather than 'him'. This is grammatically correct, but theologically misleading. In our minds and imagination it is difficult for us to conceive of the Spirit as 'him' since he has no form of his own. God has no form either, since God is spirit, yet Jesus taught us to call God 'Father', and it is not difficult for us to give some form to that reality. As far as Jesus is concerned, although we have neither photograph nor sculpture of him, there are some very human, biographical details available to us about him in the gospels of the New Testament. In the Trinity then, of Father, Son and Holy Spirit, we can cope in our minds with the persons of the Father and the Son, but we struggle with the person of the Holy Spirit. The problem is compounded by the fact that inanimate elements – wind, fire, oil – are used to describe and define him in the Bible. All of these lead to the difficulty of our recognising the Holy Spirit as a person.

If we are going to grasp the Holy Spirit's real significance, we need to dwell on the reality that he is a person. In the beginning God said 'let us make man in our image, in our likeness. . .' The Hebrew word for God which is used about thirty times in the first chapters of Genesis is *Elohim* – a plural noun. This is the reason for that unusual, though accurate translation. *Elohim* embodies the fact that God is three persons. So the Holy Spirit is at one with the Father and the Son – he has personality as they do. In the New Testament a frequent word used to refer to the Holy Spirit is the Greek word *parakletos* which comes from two Greek words *para* + *kaleō* put together. *Para* means 'alongside of' whilst *kaleō* means 'I call'. Literally it can be translated 'someone who is called alongside to help'. It is used normally in a legal context of an advocate or a counsellor in the lawcourts. It is always used of people. Jesus himself speaks of sending the disciples 'another Counsellor' in response to the pleading sadness of their hearts at the prospect of his leaving them. The word he uses for 'another' in this context is the Greek word *allos*. There are two Greek words for 'another' – *allos* and *heteros*. *Allos* means: 'another of the same kind' whilst *heteros* means: 'another of a different kind'. What Jesus is really promising is that 'another of the same kind as he is' will come to be with them for ever. As they have known, loved, appreciated and depended on him as a warm, loving companion, so it will be with the Holy Spirit. The New Testament very clearly gives personal attributes to the Holy Spirit. For example, it speaks of the mind of the Spirit, the love of the Spirit, the Spirit being grieved, the Spirit forbidding a course of action, the Spirit leading in one direction rather than another, the Spirit teaching man what he ought to learn. All of these, and others besides, presuppose that the Holy Spirit is a person.

Significantly, for the greater part of Jesus' ministry he rarely mentions the Holy Spirit. The main emphasis of that early ministry is that he is God's gift to those who specifically ask for him. Jesus taught: 'If you then, though you are evil, know how to give good gifts to your children, how much more will your Father in heaven give the Holy Spirit to those who ask him!' But on the eve of his passion, Jesus pours out his heart to his disciples about the Holy Spirit. Twenty-five per cent of the fourth Gospel is devoted to that last night Jesus had with his disciples. He is impressing upon them so many needful things to be grasped about the Holy Spirit. There is tension and apprehension in the air as he speaks of these fundamental things in relation to the Holy Spirit. This teaching is going to have a profound and eminently practical effect upon them in the years that lie ahead. Before Jesus came, all that the disciples had to offer to people in need was sympathy. During the time that Jesus was with them that changed. They were able to serve people with reality and effectiveness. They met needs as they arose. They answered questions as they were asked. Now they feared, as Jesus spoke of his departure, that when he left them they would return to the human impotence which could only offer sympathy in the face of the crying needs of men and women. As I entered into the concerns and emotions of these disciples as they contemplated the departure of their Master, I noted many things and I began to summarise them. Here they are:

1. The self-same Spirit that had been given to the Son would be given to them.

2. The Holy Spirit would be to them all that he had been to him.

3. The Holy Spirit would be to them all that the Son had been to them – and more.

4. The Holy Spirit would be in them, as the Son had been with them.

5. They would gain in the Holy Spirit more than they would lose in the departure of Christ.

6. He would be 'another of the same kind' as Christ – and, through his indwelling Christ would live in them.

7. The Holy Spirit's mission was to glorify the Son by taking the things of Christ and making them available to us. His concern is that Christ's character would be formed in us – so he imparts his fruit to us. And his concern is that Christ's conduct would be shown by us – so he imparts his gifts to us. His ministry is to produce the Jesus-life in us.

Clearly there is no competition or conflict among the Father, Son and Holy Spirit. What God the Father sent God the Son into the world to make possible by his death and resurrection, God the Holy Spirit came into the world to make actual. However, Jesus had to leave the disciples and return to his Father, and allow his disciples to await the event of Pentecost before they were to become fully aware of what he really meant on that last momentous night with them when he said: 'But I am telling you the truth: it is better for you that I go away, because if I do not go, the Helper will not come to you. But if I go away, then I will send him to you.' So other servants of the Lord have discovered that in practice to be a Christian is not difficult, it is impossible – apart from the provision God has made by his Spirit.

One of the greatest privileges that God has ever given me was the share on the pastoral staff of our church for two all-too-short years with the former missionary leader and statesman, Len Moules. Len was a former army major who had seen active service in North Africa during World War II, and had been a missionary in the hostile terrain of the Tibetan Border for many years. Inevitably he became the Field Leader and ultimately the Home and International Director of his Mission, the Worldwide Evangelisation Crusade. It was out of this rich background of experience that Len joined us. For me it was a curious Paul and Timothy relationship since Paul insisted on being Timothy. Only a short time before the Lord quite unexpectedly called Len home, he shared his experience of Pentecost publicly. It was a crisis time in his life and he tells it in this way:

I had my head in my hands up in my office in Highland Road, Upper Norwood, Crystal Palace. I'd come to the end of my tether. I could not go on. I felt like giving up, and yet was reluctant to do that.

At that time there had come into the candidates course a young man called Jim. And when that young man came in, with him came a dimension of spiritual life that I have very seldom known since. I loved to hear Jim pray and share, and when he wasn't praying or sharing, he walked about as the very essence of Jesus himself. That candidate had a dimension of spiritual power I didn't have. And

here I was, British Secretary, with twenty years missionary experience under my belt. I sat one night with my
head in my hands, and the Holy Spirit said to me,

'Call for Jim.'

'Sorry, Lord, what did you say?'

'Call for Jim.'

'But, Lord, the British Secretary doesn't call for a
candidate to give him spiritual counselling.'

'Call for Jim.'

'Yes, Lord, I know he could help, bless him – but
there is position, there is status, Lord. You don't ask
candidates to pray with British Secretaries.'

'Call for Jim.'

We had an internal phone so I dialled down to a room
below.

'Is Jim about?' Of course, God had arranged for Jim
to be about. He was going to help. Jim walked into my
office, and as a big brother to a little brother I poured
out my heart to him. Jim was young, a candidate, yet so
mature. When I'd finished, with my head in my hands,
he said, 'Let's pray.' The next moments are sacred; I
don't like to share them with anybody. But they concluded with a touch from his hands on my head, and a
prayer of such Holy Ghost initiation came from his lips
that an experience of fire went through me. God met me
that night in a new dimension of his Holy Spirit.

His biographer writes:

It was a different Len that rose from his knees that
evening – an ordinary man who had experienced an extraordinary touch from God. It was so real and so vital
that he confessed that 'even his position in the mission
would have to take second place to the light the Lord
had given and the blessing he had been granted'. From
that day Len knew without a shadow of doubt that the
filling and gifts of the Holy Spirit set out in the Scriptures
were God's provision for his own as they lived in the
world. A new power, a new authority, and a new anointing entered Len's experience.

God has no favourites – not even one so choice as Len Moules – and this is his provision for all his servants. This is normal Christianity. Jesus chose twelve disciples – eleven of whom were to become the spearhead of the dramatic influence of the Church as it spread from Jerusalem to Rome in about thirty years, affecting everything and everyone as it went. In the thrilling record of the Acts of the Apostles, they and their companions are called *agrammatoi idiotēs* ('ungrammatical idiots' – if you want a very loose translation!) In the light of subsequent discovery, it is clear that Jesus did not call them because they were more religious or more spiritual than others within their contemporary society. Indeed, it is surprising that Jesus called them at all. In 1948 the discovery of the Dead Sea Scrolls in some caves in Israel revealed that there were groups of people living in 'monasteries' throughout Judea during the time of Jesus on earth – the Essenes. Their lives were given to prayer, fasting, and studying the Scriptures. That would have seemed a much more promising pool for Jesus to fish in for companions and disciples. However, it was not to these rarified 'theological colleges' that Jesus went, but to the bustling sea-shore of Galilee and the busy thoroughfares of commercial, political and social life. The disciples he did call and appoint as apostles were inexperienced, uneducated for the most part, poor artisans with calloused hands and weatherbeaten skin. It is a salutory reminder that God does not choose us or anyone else for what we are, but for what we are not. Such, indeed, has been the way of God throughout history.

The great Old Testament leader, Moses, spent forty years learning to be somebody. He was educated in the wisdom and learning of the rich Egyptian culture. I have an uncanny feeling every time I pass Cleopatra's Needle on the Thames Embankment in London. It was one of the ornate gateposts of the University of Heliopolis which Moses almost certainly would have attended as a young man. Did Moses actually pass Cleopatra's Needle there each day as he went to his classes? However, the next forty years he spent in the desert looking after his father-in-law's sheep – and learning to be a nobody. It takes a long time and is a wearying process to unlearn the deep-seated conviction that we are better than others. Moses spent the remaining forty years of his life being a very effective servant of the Lord – and realising, almost daily, what God can do with a nobody (and that at eighty years of age and onwards).

The Holy Spirit is the one who wants to take the seemingly irrelevant nobodies and make them relevant to the unfolding of the purposes of God within the Body of Christ, the Church. The relevant question is not: 'Do you speak in tongues?' but rather: 'Are you really convinced that you are becoming an effective member of the Body of Christ?'

The time has long since past for us to keep on asking the question: 'What shall I call this reality?' or 'When does it happen?' The questions that need to press themselves upon us are: 'Is this reality for me?' and 'What effect does it have in my life?' We need to stop quibbling about the terms which are used and start anticipating and experiencing the reality of which they speak.

In the Bible such phrases as 'I will send upon you what my Father has promised'; 'power from above comes down upon you'; 'wait for the gift I told you about, the gift my Father promised'; 'baptised with the Holy Spirit'; 'filled with power'; 'receive God's gift'; 'filled with the Holy Spirit'; 'the Spirit enabled them'; 'God has poured out his gift of the Holy Spirit'; 'God gave those Gentiles the same gift'; all add up to a very exciting summary.

First, the Bible indicates clearly that the Holy Spirit has come not to make Christians happy, but to make them useful and effective. He came not for our enjoyment, but to make us employable. Jesus spoke about the Baptism in the Holy Spirit in the context of living life effectively in the Kingdom of God. He said that the basic need of the disciples was 'power from above' and this is what he promises to make sure that they will possess – they would be 'filled with power'. The word for 'power' – *dunamis* – may also be translated 'ability'. So it was with 'power' or 'ability' that the disciples witnessed, testified and served the Lord. The ministry of the Holy Spirit is to enable us to be part of the fulfilling of the Christian prayer which Jesus taught his disciples to pray: 'Thy kingdom come. Thy will be done on earth as it is in heaven.'

Secondly, we are left in no doubt that the provision of God the Holy Spirit is in abundance and not in short supply. For example, the word 'baptism' means to plunge, immerse totally, or completely envelop. It was used of ships which sunk or, commercially, for the dying of fabrics. There is something very comprehensive and total about the concept. Again, when we speak about 'filling' something we are thinking about completeness. The other word which speaks of the profusion of God's provision is 'poured out'. It does not signify a God who is calculating or niggardly – concerned about apportioning the more or the less. There is the heady atmosphere of prodigality about God's involvement of us in the life of the Spirit.

Thirdly, we are reminded that the one who 'provides' the Spirit is God himself. He is 'from above'; 'comes down'; 'comes upon'; he is indeed 'God's gift'. He cannot be earned by anyone, nor can he be bestowed by any man. We can only receive with grateful hearts what God wants to give. He is the result of grace and mercy in the heart of God. In the context of the Holy Spirit, one of the loveliest words in the New Testament has been appropriated and, sadly, has often been used carelessly. I am referring to the word 'charismatic'. It comes from that lovely New Testament word *charis* which is normally translated 'grace'. Grace is the sheer undeserved generosity of the heart of God. It is the very essence of the Christian Gospel. So significant and precious is it that Paul begins and ends each of his letters which have been included in the New Testament scriptures with it. For him it was the foundation reality of all that made life significant. The word *charisma* is normally translated 'a gift' (sometimes of the Holy Spirit) while the word *charismata* is the plural of that word – that is, 'gifts' (sometimes of the Holy Spirit). I prefer to think of *charisma(ta)* as the manifestation(s) of God's sheer undeserved generosity. Such is the calling upon every member of the family of

God. Such is the concern of God that this would be so that his Spirit has been poured forth to enable us to do just that.

Fourthly, the terms which are used in relation to the Holy Spirit and the context in which they are used remind us of the people who are to experience and enjoy the provision of God – the Gentile as well as the Jew; and those who are living now as well as those who were part of the ongoing work of God then. The power and the ability of God is available for us now today.

Here is a prayer which has been a great help to many within our Fellowship as we have used it within our 'Life in the Spirit' Seminars:

Lord Jesus Christ I want to spend what remains of my life fulfilling your purposes and doing your will. I want to be completely freed from any area of darkness where your light and your life has not fully penetrated. I want to live my life as an obvious citizen of the Kingdom of God and to be an effective and relevant part of the Body of Christ. I will turn away from all wrongdoing, and I will avoid everything that leads me to wrongdoing.

I ask you to forgive all the sins that I have committed.

I offer my life afresh to you, and with your help and guidance I will obey you as my Lord.

I ask you now to baptise me in the Holy Spirit, and to release me in praise in a way that I have never praised you before.

5: Evangelism – the need to reproduce

One of the unmistakeable characteristics of life is the ability to reproduce the same life which you possess. This week we have said farewell to one of our church members leaving us to nurse in Ghana and another couple going to Hong Kong to share in the ministry of a quite remarkable venture of faith to care for severely handicapped and unwanted children in the Colony. In two days time we will again be searching for car parking space at the airport as we commend yet another of our folk to the Lord as she returns for the third time to northern Ivory Coast to continue her work of Bible translation and a literacy programme under the general guidance of the Wycliffe Bible Translators. Who can tell all that is involved in these four lives – the struggle with materialism; the value of possessions; the heartbreak of separation from loved ones; the apprehension of the future; the wistful longing for the familiar and the predictable; the apprehension about a new life-style; the re-orientation to a new culture and climate; the prospect of a life of singleness; the pressures of the powers of darkness; the lack of understanding – even among mature Christians? So the list could go on and on. Why do they do it? Why does the church solemnly and lovingly pledge itself to support them totally – spiritually, physically, financially, socially, and emotionally? Why did our hearts thrill with wonder as they knelt amongst us and we laid our hands on them? Because this is the will of the Lord for them and for us. The symbol of the Christian Faith is a cross not a circle.

The world's great heart is aching, aching fiercely in the
    night,
And God alone can heal it and God alone give light;
And the men to bear that message, and to speak the
    living Word,
Are you and I, my brothers, and all others who have
    heard.

Can we close our eyes to duty? Can we fold our hands at
    ease,
While the gates of night stand open to the pathway of
    the seas?
Can we shut up our compassion, can we leave one prayer
    unsaid,
Till the lands which hell has blasted have been quickened
    from the dead?

We grovel among trifles and our spirits fret and toss,
While above us burns the vision of the Christ upon the
    Cross,
And the blood of Christ is streaming from His wounded
    hands and side;
And the lips of Christ are saying, 'Tell poor sinners I
    have died'.

O voice of God, we hear Thee, above the wrecks of Time,
Thine echoes roll around us, and the message is sublime;
No power of man shall thwart us, no stronghold shall
    dismay,
For God commands obedience, and love has led the way.

I do not know who wrote these lines – and they may not
meet the purist's concept of good poetry – but they embrace
the cry of the New Testament's heart.

There was a day when the Church was anaesthetised by
intellectual controversy; theological smugness; evangelical
individualism; social respectability; and spiritual parochi-
alism. At that time the Spirit of God was able only to stir
a few individual hearts to the needs of the whole world.
Thank God, that stirring was not mistaken and became
very productive. For example, in June 1965, young Hudson

Taylor became so burdened by God for China that he found the self-satisfied, hymn-singing Brighton congregation to which he belonged quite intolerable. He saw it as: 'Pew upon pew of prosperous, bearded merchants, shopkeepers, visitors; demure wives in bonnets and crinolines, scrubbed children trained to hide their impatience.' The atmosphere of smug piety sickened him. He seized his hat and left. He shares his heart when he says he was 'unable to bear the sight of a congregation of a thousand or more Christian people rejoicing in their own security, while millions were perishing through lack of knowledge'. He tells us that: 'he wandered out on the sands alone, in great spiritual agony'. On that same day, under the morning sun on the beach, he prayed for twenty-four willing skilful labourers. So the China Inland Mission was born (afterwards to become the Overseas Missionary Fellowship, as it is today).

We need to confront the age-old response that we do a disservice to humanity by declaring the Gospel of Christ to them, since that only makes the innocent and the unaware guilty. Nothing could be further from the truth. There is no one in the world who has not had the truth – whether they live in plushy, privately-owned, swimming-pooled suburbia or in a primitive, austere and basic jungle location. The whole emphasis of the Bible is that all have suppressed the truth that has been known about God in the created world. There are two things you can know about God without ever sitting on an uncomfortable church pew or opening the Bible; the first is that God is powerful and the second is that he is divine as distinct from human. No one, whatever his point of view, has ever attributed the world to man's creative ingenuity or ability. Unless and until we grasp this it will never be properly understood why we must take the Gospel of Christ to the whole world – the world is not innocent, but guilty before God; nor is the world ignorant of basic truth about God, but it has turned the truth down. So Christ commands us to go and share his transforming Gospel with everyone everywhere, not to change their innocence into guilt, but to confront their guilt with the forgiveness and grace of God. Archaeology has challenged the concept that man started by worshipping trees and animals, and then began to fashion idols and worship them until religions emerged which believed in one supreme God. It is not true that man began in a primitive, occult animism and graduated to a belief in one supreme God. Man, in the beginning, worshipped one supreme God and deteriorated and declined into worshipping idols of his own creation and natural phenomena which were already in his experience. It is not within the scope of this book to develop this reality. Suffice it to say that the archaeologist and the anthropologist have challenged the commonly accepted view of an evolutionary philosophy of man's spiritual development. In fact, the one thing you cannot do before God is plead either innocence or ignorance.

In past generations this task was left to the committed and sometimes thought-to-be fanatical few. As the Giant has stirred from slumber, we have wakened to the fact that God never intended it to be so. The reproduction of the Jesus life in others requires the involvement of the whole Body of Christ motivated and enabled by the power of the Holy Spirit. As we have wakened to the instruction of the Bible, we have come to realise that evangelism is not the 'thing' of the few and the lip-service of the many, but is the costly, demanding obligation of us all in one way or another. It was for this purpose that God the Holy Spirit came.

Samuel Chadwick, formerly the Principal of Cliff College reminds us that 'the Holy Ghost does not come upon methods, but upon men. He does not anoint machinery, but men. He does not work through organisations, but through men. He does not dwell in buildings, but in men. He indwells the Body of Christ, directs its activities, distributes its forces, empowers its members.' To what purpose all this activity? To credit us with the risen life of Christ so that others may come to know that reality and liberty too.

The Mission Board of our church set aside a day of prayer and fasting during which God laid the following six things on their hearts:

1. Each one of us must keep our lives open before God,

never assuming that the course of our life is fixed into its present mould. Constantly and honestly the question must be asked: 'Is there anything else the Lord wants me to do?' We have a responsibility to *listen* to the reply. (The implications of this are devastating – especially as you get older!)

2. A basic attitude in our Christian lives must be: Not, 'what can I get?' but 'what can I give?' We have a responsibility to *give*. (Every Christian believes this. Every minister preaches it. But isn't it so hard to live this way?)

3. Every young person should offer his life to God's service before he commences his university course or career of his choice; and before he becomes engaged or married. We have a responsibility to *offer ourselves without reserve*. (The implications of this are extraordinarily difficult – especially if you are young!)

4. Every church member should determine to pray many of our membership (both young and old) out and into evangelism, full-time service, and the mission field; accepting the implications of such praying. We have a responsibility to *pray*. (We have found that some of those who do pray this way become the answer to their own praying – so be warned!)

5. We must realistically face the cost of a heavy commitment in terms of personnel, prayer and finance. We have a responsibility to *sacrifice*. (How important it is to get this out of Sunday evening emotion into Monday morning reality.)

6. Our young people should feel free to approach their leaders, or other leaders, to ask them what they should be doing *now* in order to prepare themselves for the eventual call of God. We have a responsibility to *train*. (Everything these days seems to be going 'instant' – instant coffee; instant credit; instant purchasing; instant blessings. It is irritating to us to discover that God is not in a hurry. He can create a saint in an instant, but it takes him quite a time to build a servant – in the case of Moses forty years; in the case of Jesus eighteen years; in the case of the disciples three years.)

It is one thing hearing God say these things. It is quite

another to live individually and corporately as if he had said them. So we are discovering together. There is a lurking wistful hope that God did not mean it after all. Without question, God's desire for the Body of Christ is that it would grow. I sense sometimes an underlying defensiveness against growth in the Church. There seems to be a quick desire to rationalise failure to grow. There is a basic honesty in the attitude that faces either a 'plateau' experience or decline by asking questions why this is so. It is, however, a strange phenomenon that enables us to come to the conclusion that God is pleased when churches year after year and generation after generation remain static or decline in numbers and effectiveness. It is biblical and theological nonsense to argue in this way, and to maintain that position. Some who hold it set growth against godliness, and choose to emphasise the latter rather than the former. Others maintain that if we emphasise new conversions too much we jeopardise consolidation within the church. Those who want to take this view of evangelism often turn to the strategy of Gideon in the Old Testament and the loneliness of Jesus on the cross in the New Testament. However true it is that Gideon indeed reduced his 32,000 volunteers to 300 in order to attack the Midianites so successfully, the fact remains that for each example of Gideon's battle strategy, the Bible has many more examples of Joshua's style which threw as many as possible into the thick of the fight.

In the same way – although it hardly bears comparison – to justify non-evangelism on the grounds that although Jesus drew great crowds to listen to his preaching, it required a conscript to carry his cross, and he ultimately died a lonely death on Calvary, is hardly tenable.

Jesus condenses the purpose of his coming into the world into that simple and familiar sentence: 'For the Son of Man came to seek and to save what was lost.' Jesus came not only to reveal God to man, but also to redeem man to God. If that was so during the years of his incarnation, can it be altered by his body on earth today? Jesus was concerned enough about statistics to affirm that the love of the Father's heart was touched when one sheep was missing out of a flock of one hundred. That love would not be satisfied until that sheep was found and returned to safety. Here is a source of joy in heaven.

Jesus declared quite categorically: 'I will build my church, and the gates of Hades will not overcome it' (or 'will not prove stronger than it'). The implication is that nothing can cramp or retard its growth – not even the organised hierarchy of evil! Jesus speaks about the Kingdom of God (or the rule or government of God) a great deal. In fact it is his main theme in preaching – 116 times in the Gospel of Mark and Luke. It is the last word which the apostle Paul proclaimed. It is the reality which the Church is commissioned to declare. Jesus compares the Kingdom of God to a grain of mustard seed – so small that the naked eye can barely detect it. Yet locked inside that tiny seed is a tree which can grow anything from eight to twelve feet tall. It looks so frail, insignificant and small, and yet has within it this potential for incredible growth. So with the Church.

It is true that Jesus did end up on a cross. It is true that his disciples had either abandoned him or were so afraid of identification with him that they kept their distance. Yet Jesus died in order that the work of the devil might be destroyed; ordinary people set free; soiled, frustrated, failing human beings made new creatures; new members be added to the living, functioning Body of Christ. Jesus began by calling twelve people to himself. At the end of three years – the time which had elapsed between the start and the finish of his active ministry – that twelve had become a committed group of 120 disciples. Perhaps it would be more accurate to estimate the number in terms of upwards of 500 – as hinted in 1 Corinthians 15:6. Growth from 12 to 120 in 3 years represents an annual growth rate of 115 per cent. That is impressive enough without reckoning on the figure of 500 rather than 120.

It may well be argued that the smaller the number at the start the more impressive the percentage of growth. Can it be sustained? Was it continued? The strategy was not to go about the business of reducing the 120 to a 'Gideon's band'

– but rather Jesus was concerned that all 120 were filled with the Holy Spirit and praised God in a tongue which was not familiar to them. They proclaimed the Gospel of Christ in the power of the Holy Spirit, and about 3,000 were added to the Church. This would seem to be a much more accurate description of God's will for a healthy church than the story of Gideon or the dark, destructive moments on Calvary. 120 to 3,120 in one day is quite impressive evangelism! Clearly those involved used their spiritual gifts and cared for the new converts with the result that Pentecost became a daily experience. So significant was the growth rate that the authorities became alarmed and tried to silence Peter and John – but not before another 5,000 had been won to Christ. At this point a minimum estimate of statistics would ensure that about 8,120 were now part of the living, growing Church. The Jerusalem church grew so rapidly that precise figures became impossible. But by the time of Acts 6 and the impact of persecution the Church had grown from the original 120 to something in excess of 10,000. It really does make laughable the constant frowning protestations of many within a thriving local church situation: 'We are getting too big now!' How big is too big? Small may well be beautiful – but how blessed is it to remain that way?

The 'romantic' story of Acts continues with Philip the evangelist – who in all probability had not even been a Christian when Jesus was crucified – being forced out of Jerusalem because of persecution, and planting churches in Samaria. These churches grew in an embarrassing way since the life of God appeared to be no respecter of persons – even though the Samaritans were traditionally despised by the Jews.

By the time the Gospel of Christ had reached Galilee Luke, who began by recording that *people* were first added, and then multiplied, is now speaking of *churches* being multiplied. This corporate emphasis continues not only in terms of *churches*, but in terms of whole *communities* turning to the Lord – 'all those who lived at Lydda and Sharon saw him and turned to the Lord'.

So from Jews to Samaritans and ultimately to Gentiles. The political situation put immense pressure on evangelising among the Jews before the first century was over, but what began at Antioch among the Gentiles has continued and indeed has accelerated right into the twentieth century.

Towards the end of the apostle Paul's life – whose call from God was to evangelise and plant churches among the Gentiles – the number of Jews who had become Christians could be estimated only in terms of multiples of thousands.

Not only did Jesus die for Church growth, and command Church growth, but he left an extraordinary example of Church growth through his ministry. God's work in the world today will never be accomplished by timid, retreating, pessimistic people who rationalise defeat, but only by those who recognise that God is looking for lives that are totally open and responsive to him in reality, which he can fill with his Holy Spirit and which are prepared to face the tears, misunderstanding, and heart-ache of such abandonment.

Some months ago, as a result of the policy of our church Mission Board, I spent a few days in Hong Kong. During this time I heard of the work of Jackie Pullinger for the first time. While I was there I began to read the book about her ministry. Apart from the fascinating story which is told there, my own spirit was 'quickened' (I don't like the word, but I don't know how else to express the experience) by her testimony of how the Lord dealt with her in the area of evangelism. She tells of her frustration of being aware that there is a dimension of power which was awesomely effective in the New Testament and significantly relevant today among some, and the plausible explanations of others, both theological and practical, why God does not and cannot work that way now. She identifies in a Chinese couple the 'something' that she is looking for, and their sensitivity and care for her to enable her to find it. Their ministry is followed by the disappointment of her not experiencing what they had anticipated in the way that they had anticipated it. A year of disillusionment followed in that nothing significant had really happened to change her Christian life.

Jackie Pullinger speaks of her reaction to it all as 'being cheated'. One year after this experience with the Chinese couple she is introduced to an American couple who speak very forthrightly to her about praying in tongues. She does not deny the reality of this gift, but dismisses it as hardly relevant to her situation. The Americans encouraged her to begin again to use her prayer language and then to go on praying in the language of the Spirit every day (for fifteen minutes by the clock). After a period of six weeks she began to notice that those she talked to about Jesus Christ responded and believed. As ever, as a human being, she sought a human explanation for this divine phenomenon – had her Chinese dramatically improved or had she unconsciously begun to adopt a new evangelistic technique? Appraisal of her situation convinced her that what had changed was that now she was talking about Jesus to people who were prepared to listen and actually wanted to hear. As she allowed God – however foolish the means appeared to her – to have his way in her prayers, it produced a dramatic and direct result. She was discovering that prayer is not me getting God to do what I want; nor is prayer God getting me to do what he wants; but prayer is me getting God to do what God wants. Our reasonable and logical minds respond to that by concluding that it is irrelevant to see prayer in this way since God will accomplish what he wants anyway, since he is sovereign. However, the Bible holds in perfect balance divine sovereignty and human responsibility; and with regard to prayer teaches: 'You have not, because you do not ask for it.' Jackie Pullinger testifies clearly that now she began to find that person after person wanted to receive Jesus as Lord and Saviour. Her own heart responded in humility and wonder that God would allow her to have even a small part in his ongoing work. She began to see that he was doing miracles in the world today – in all kinds of unmistakeable ways – but that the greatest miracle of all occurs when a life 'fast bound in sin and nature's night' is set free by Jesus to become a member of the family of God and a citizen in God's Kingdom.

Years ago D. L. Moody had his own Pentecost which

affected not only his life in the midst of the years, but lives of countless thousands for all eternity. His son, W. R. Moody, records the event in his father's own words:

> One day in New York – oh, what a day! – I cannot describe it. I seldom refer to it: it is almost too sacred an experience to name. I can only say God revealed himself to me and I had such an experience of his love that I had to ask him to stay his hand. I went to preaching again. The sermons were not different, and yet hundreds were converted. I would not now be placed back where I was before that blessed experience if you should give me all the world.

It is so easy to be critical. It is so human to want everything neatly tabulated and filed away in self-contained theological pigeon-holes. It is so traditional to divide into theological camps and view others with suspicion, if not with hostility. But all the time the great heart of God is aching over his unredeemed world while he has given us Good News to declare and the resources, authority, and opportunity to proclaim it.

I am convinced that, especially in evangelism, we need to review and then adopt in the twentieth century the 'methods' of evangelism lived out so effectively in the first century by a Church which was far from perfect and yet was touching spiritual reality in a way that we know only minimally. There were four main contributing factors.

1. The power which Jesus promised and then provided for his disciples by the Holy Spirit

Without this all else assumes a muted irrelevance. In the same climate of mystified confusion that so often characterises the Western Church today in the face of the plain word of Scripture and the straightforward promises of God, Luke tells us: 'Then he (Jesus) opened their minds so they could understand the Scriptures. He told them, "This is what is written: The Christ will suffer and rise again on the third day, and repentance and forgiveness of sins will be preached in his name to all nations, beginning at Jerusalem.

You are witnesses of these things. I am going to send you what my Father has promised, but stay in the city until you have been clothed with power from on high" ' (Luke 24:45–7). We argue, debate and discuss this reality. When does it happen? What shall we call it? How does it manifest itself? Who should possess it? Is it for now as well as then?

David Winter once wrote: 'In the institutional, moribund, introverted ranks of our Christian churches, we have a private dialogue with ourselves while man plunges suicidally on into absurdity and despair.' Just so! The point is that either we have this power or we do not. Certainly the early Church had it. Certainly we were intended to have it: 'The promise is for you (those Jews who were present when Peter preached in Jerusalem) and your children (the next generation) and for all who are far off (those spread throughout the world – Gentiles as well as Jews) – for all whom the Lord our God will call (referring to future generations who would know the Kingdom life of God)' (Acts 2:39).

It is important to notice that it was not the resurrection of Jesus which gave power to the early disciples and drove out their fear. They were fearfully huddled behind locked doors on that first Easter night when Jesus came to them. They were still huddled behind locked doors for fear of the authorities one week later. It was not the resurrection which transformed cowards into martyrs – the resurrection gave them great joy – but it was Pentecost which gave them great power and courage: 'When they saw the courage of Peter and John and realised that they were unschooled, ordinary men, they were astonished and took note that these men had been with Jesus' (Acts 4:13). This was the impact these disciples had on the clinical, hard-nosed, religious authorities. On their release, under threat of punishment, they were at it again as a corporate body: '. . . they were all filled with the Holy Spirit and spoke the word of God boldly.' The same thing characterised the ministry of Paul after Ananias had laid his hands on him to be filled with the Holy Spirit. In the very place where he was known as an opponent of Christ he preached the message of Christ in power. Barnabas in commending Paul says: '. . . in Damascus he had preached fearlessly in the name of Jesus'.

Not only did the Holy Spirit have a profound effect on God's servants, but also on those to whom they went. As a result of Peter's preaching in the power of the Holy Spirit 'the people . . . were cut to the heart'. So also with Paul: 'as Paul discoursed on righteousness, self-control, and the judgment to come, Felix was afraid. . .' So often today when we preach people congratulate us or politely acknowledge what has been said. There is a lack of penetration and spiritual force in our preaching.

Then, again, the miraculous, the supernatural, accompanied their preaching. Those in demonic bondage were set free; those physically sick and crippled were healed; there were miracles of judgment as well as blessing. God was seen to confirm his word with unmistakeable signs – visions, prophecies, signs and wonders. A miracle is three things at once. It is a natural event which takes place in the sphere of nature. It is an unnatural event in that it cuts across natural, normal laws. It is a supernatural event in that it is caused from outside nature itself – from God. So a miracle is a natural event which follows an unnatural course and has a supernatural cause or origin. On page after page of Acts there is not only the powerful and effective proclamation of the word of God there is also the demonstration of the power of God. These two go together.

2. *There was constant praying in the Church*

They prayed to receive power to begin with; and having received it they lived in the climate of prayer to retain the power they had received. In twenty of the twenty-eight chapters of Acts prayer is mentioned. They prayed in the night and at the breaking of the day; they prayed in the storm as well as in the calm; they prayed in the prison cell and on the seashore; they prayed when they were persecuted and when they were dying. They prayed over their converts and over the sick. They prayed when they appointed apostles, elders and deacons. So prayer was almost like the air that they breathed – a life support system for effectiveness.

Martin Luther said: 'If I fail to spend two hours in prayer each morning, the devil gets the victory through the day.' That is as may be, and to follow the pattern of another man slavishly ends in spiritual barrenness and death. But nevertheless it does make the point that 'What a man is alone on his knees before God, *that* he is – and no more.' That is true not only of the individual, but also of the corporate Body of Christ. 'What a Church is together on its knees before God, *that* it is – and no more.' However searingly sore this makes our conscience, humbling us and often haunting us with guilt, the fact remains and will not go away. Maybe this is why we say it so often, even though the response remains meagre, the fact is that it is true. Samuel Chadwick, whose life presents me with a constant challenge, said: 'Though a man should have all knowledge of prayer, and though he understands all mysteries about prayer, unless he prays he will never learn to pray. That man who prays is irresistible, and the devil knows it.' Prayer is the heart of evangelism.

3. There was powerful preaching in the early Church
Luke, in Acts, uses a whole variety of words to describe how it was done: they preached, heralded, entreated, proclaimed, disputed, reasoned, persuaded – and so on. They did it where they could – in homes, prisons, courts, lecture halls, chariots, the Temple and synagogues – wherever and whenever they could, they did!

Years ago, as real interest in the Church began to stir within me, I can remember being fascinated by articles which used to appear in the Saturday Glasgow Evening Citizen newspaper by a man called Alexander Gammie. These competed with my priority interest in the Sports section of the paper. At one time, apparently, Alexander Gammie was touring some of the Scottish churches, making his own observations, and then publicly purveying his reactions (I should imagine it must have been a spiritual desert time for him!). He told in one article of a fashionable

church he had just visited. He described the storied architecture, the soul-melting music, the crowded congregation,
the atmosphere of happy comradeship, the tone of
workman-like efficiency which characterised everything
that was done. Last of all he gave his personal reaction to
the preacher: 'There is an air of experience about him, and
there is certainly nothing hesitant about his manner in the
pulpit. He has also an assurance which seems to carry him
through a service without any sign of his being unduly
oppressed by the burden of his office.' I am not sure to this
day what he meant since any task undertaken and accomplished in the power of the Holy Spirit gives an exhilarating
freedom which is quite unique and distinguishable from
any other human experience. Yet maybe he did mean that
there seemed to be an unawareness that he was co-operating
with God in one of the most remarkable miracles that affects
men and women. So preaching is the means God uses to
transform lives and to secure eternity for countless millions.
Lord Eustace Percy at the beginning of this century, said:
'To think of changing the world by changing the people in
it might be an act of great faith; but talk of changing the
world without changing the people in it is an act of lunacy.'

Preaching the word of God under the anointing of the
Holy Spirit is the means God uses to change people. Film
services, spectacular testimonies, dialogues, discussions,
charismatic worship, interviews, drama, etc. may well have
their place, but always in addition to or as an accompaniment to the preaching of the Word of God.

We set ourselves the task in our church of making a
summary of the essential content of what we preach, and
came up with something like this:

> God created us to love, so that we might respond in love
> to Him. Because he wants us to find and serve the true
> God, he brings us under his government so that our lives
> can be properly controlled and directed. This will enable
> us to become the people he created us to be.
>
> We are spiritually dead, however, because of our sin
> and rebellion and cannot respond to him. We are spiri-

tually blind, and consequently do not see the need and cannot find the way to respond to his love.

God has taken the initiative and has come to us by his Holy Spirit, making us aware of our dilemma and enabling us to repent and believe on the Lord Jesus Christ. Our only hope is focused on Jesus Christ, who died in our place on the cross, becoming sin on our behalf and bearing the wrath of God against sin. He rose from the dead, ascended into heaven, poured out his Holy Spirit upon the Church, and now prays for us.

We are transferred from the Kingdom of darkness to the Kingdom of God's Son, not by anything we do, but because of what he has done by his grace. This becomes real for us through faith in Christ.

Jesus puts us into a right relationship with God; puts God's divine life within us in abundant measure by his Holy Spirit; and assures us that physical death is not the end, but a new beginning with God.

Such is the richness and relevance of what we have to say as the messengers of God.

4. There is the priority of evangelism in the Church programme

'Those who had been scattered preached the word wherever they went.' 'Now those who had been scattered by the persecution in connection with Stephen travelled as far as Phoenicia, Cyprus and Antioch, telling the message only to Jews. Some of them, however, men from Cyprus and Cyrene, went to Antioch and began to speak to Greeks also, telling them the Good News about the Lord Jesus. The Lord's hand was with them and a great number of people believed and turned to the Lord.' F. B. Meyer commenting on this says: 'Antioch will ever be famous in Christian annals because a number of unordained and unlearned disciples dared to preach the Gospel.'

Gibbon, the historian, said of these first Christians that: 'It became the most sacred duty of the new convert to diffuse among his friends the unmistakeable blessing which he had received.'

The crusty Scotsman, Thomas Carlyle, confirms that observation: 'How did Christianity arise? Not by institutions and well-ordered systems. It arose in the mystic deep of a man's soul and was spread by simple and individual effort, and flew like a hallowed fire from heart to heart.'

It was for this purpose that the Holy Spirit was given that ordinary men and women should be willing and effective witnesses in ever-widening circles which ultimately would embrace the whole world. God's heart will be satisfied not when churches are filled with God's people, but when God's people are filled with the Holy Spirit and go out into the world with boldness and relevance, demonstrating the naturally supernatural life which they declare, and so affirming that it is true that Jesus is the same today as he was yesterday – alive, compassionate and effective before the challenges of a lost human race. W. Graham Scroggie once said:

> Science has no Gospel: it moves in the realm of things behind phenomena and, at best, only gazes at truth; it cannot tell how a ruined race may be recovered. The religions of the world have no Gospel; they postulate the need of man, display the yearning of man, and enjoin endless ways and means whereby man may find the ultimate good, but they cannot give peace to the troubled heart, or joy to the songless soul. The warrant, therefore, for evangelism, is in the power of the Gospel to do what nothing else can do.

6: Fellowship – fearfully and wonderfully made

St Augustine once said: 'Men go abroad to wonder at the height of mountains, at the huge waves of the sea, at the long courses of the rivers, at the vast compass of the ocean, at the circular motion of the stars; and they pass by themselves without wondering.'

So it may be said about the Body of Christ. We have lived so long with the Church that its make-up as originally intended by God; its reality of growth and development today; the expression of the life it contains; causes little reaction of awe and wonder, and little concern to examine it to check out that it is functioning as originally intended. Wherever the Church is stirring to life again, there is always, without any exceptions, a new dawning of the delicate, intimate, tender and yet strong and resiliant associations and relationships which make its life possible. We speak of this as the miracle of fellowship.

Unfortunately, like many other words in our language, 'fellowship' has become debased. In society, for example, most people have a very vague concept of what they mean by the word 'love'. It can mean anything really from Hollywood sentimentalism with its strong overtones of sexual gratification, however speedy and furtive, however selfish and undisciplined, to the dying of Jesus of Nazareth upon the cross on the hill of Golgotha. So in the Church, fellowship is regarded and spoken of with equal vagueness and resulting confusion.

Fellowship is one of the great words of the New Testament. The psalmist is filled with wonder and praise as he considers his own body. 'I praise you', he says, 'because I am fearfully and wonderfully made; your works are wonderful, I know that full well.' He is impressed by the intricacy and yet the strength; the vulnerability and yet the resilience; the durability and yet the transience; the comprehensiveness and yet the functional appropriateness of his physical body. Fellowship is applicable to all of these wonders in the Body of Christ. In classical Greek *koinonia* ('fellowship') means 'an association' or 'a partnership'. Later, it came to mean the opposite of *pleonexia* which is the grasping, acquisitive spirit which is out for everything and anything it can get for itself. It is the embodiment and expression of general sharing as contrasted with the spirit of selfish getting. In the 'back-street' Greek of the day *koinonia* would frequently be used in the context of a business partnership, or a marriage, or a man's relationship to the gods.

It is out of this rich social background of a close, warm, personal, intimate relationship between man and man, man and woman, and the human and the divine, that *koinonia* comes. The abstract noun (*koinonia* – 'fellowship') occurs eighteen times in the New Testament. The verb (*koinonein* – 'to share' or 'to have a share in') occurs eight times in the New Testament period. The personal noun (*koinonos* – 'a partner' or 'an associate' or 'a companion' or 'a joint-owner') occurs ten times in the New Testament. To follow these words through in the New Testament within the context in which they are used is to discover some far reaching significances.

1. Fellowship is an inescapable and intrinsic part of salvation

The reality and depth of our relationship with God will be seen and can be monitored in the reality and depth of our relationships with others in the family of God. You cannot have one without the other. The vertical relationship we claim with God will be declared to us and to others more eloquently in our horizontal relationships with the other members of the Body of Christ than in all the creeds we recite, all the hymns that we sing, and all the testimonies we give. The parable of the wheel operates with an almost frightening accuracy – the closer the spokes come to the hub the closer they come to one another. So with God and his Family. I have often felt that we try to be much more spiritual than God is, as we try to spiritualise what he demands must be 'humanised'.

2. *Fellowship will always express itself in practical sharing*

Of the eight times the verb *koinonein* occurs in the New Testament, on four occasions it deals with this practical aspect of things – sharing visible, material, tangible things. The man in whom the Spirit of God really dwells cannot bear the reality that he has while others have not – and does something significant about it rather than feeling guilty over it, and making endless explanations to himself and to others why the disparity must remain. The Communist takes the attitude: 'what is yours is mine' whereas the Christian actively responds in a practical way to: 'what is mine is ours'.

If you really want to glorify God – give all you have to God; receive all God wants to give to you; and then share all God has given with others. This releases me from giving what I have to others – which so quickly leads to a proud spirit and an unhealthy relationship. The key to sharing in the Spirit is in me giving what I have to God (so that it no longer is mine, nor do I ever have any more claim on it) – and then sharing all that God gives with others.

Within our church, for many years now, we have set ourselves the task of asking three questions:

What does it mean to love one another as Christ loves us?

What does it mean to have all things common?

What does it mean to lay down your life for the brethren?

I would love to be able to write that we have at last answered these questions satisfactorily and are now living in the reality of the conclusions we have reached. Sadly I cannot do so. Sometimes, indeed, I feel we are in some areas further away from the answer than we used to be! It would be dishonest of me to make such a claim. However, our quest continues in order that we might unlock the distinctive and unique treasure of Christian fellowship. Without this there is no reality in the Giant's life.

3. Fellowship is constantly associated with serving

James and John are Peter's *koinonoi* ('partners' or 'associates') in the fishing business. Paul describes Titus as his *koinonos* and *sunergos* i.e. his 'partner and fellow-worker'. We complement, supplement, contribute to the work and service of others in order that the Body of Christ might function properly. 'In all my prayers for all of you, I always pray with joy because of your partnership (*koinonia*) in the gospel from the first day until now.'

This, too, lies at the heart of it all. As in my human body there are severe limitations on what any separate part of it can do, yet as that part submits to the directions given by the head and submissively co-operates with the other related parts, my body moves and functions as intended in a relevant way. So it is in the Body of Christ.

4. Fellowship is always related to and dependent on our relationship with the Holy Spirit

No matter how sensitive, devout, and compassionate a man may be, there are significant limits in every human relationship. How much we need to discover what it means to enjoy and experience fellowship with the Holy Spirit. Years ago I was driving to choose some furniture for my office at the church, when my companion that morning asked me quite unexpectedly: 'Do you pray to the Holy Spirit?' No one had ever asked me that before, and I do not think I had ever thought about it very seriously. It did occur to me, however, that some of our most moving and personal hymns are addressed to the Holy Spirit. My answer to my friend in the car was 'Yes.' Subsequently I have thought a good deal more about the question. Because the Holy Spirit is a person – and, indeed, the person 'called alongside to help me' – inevitably I speak with him in happy fellowship.

The relationships God intends us to have within the body

of his Son are not just natural; and they are certainly never intended to be unnatural; they are supernatural. Their reality cannot be expressed or explained in human terms because they are in a different dimension of reality. They are the result of our fellowship with the Holy Spirit.

5. Fellowship finds its unique expression in our relationship with Jesus

A Christian is someone who not only confesses that Jesus is Lord, but also believes in his heart that God raised him from the dead. Our belief is not in some*thing* which happened two thousand years ago – however humbling and incredible that may have been – but in some*one* who is alive today. It is not just reverence for or a recollection of a great life, but a living, contemporary relationship with that life. I remember coming to the end of a two-week conference in West Africa at which I had been speaking each day. The climate, the culture, the food, the battle with the powers of darkness had all taken their toll. It was the last night of the conference and the next day I was going to travel from Ghana to Ivory Coast with one of the members of our church and her partner, to see where they worked with the Wycliffe Bible Translators about 500 miles north from the coast of the Gulf of Guinea on the edge of pretty dense jungle. I looked forward so much to sharing real fellowship with these two very dear servants of the Lord and to seeing a little of their work before going south again to speak at another conference in Abidjan. I was deeply troubled about my relevance in this situation. However, a Dutch couple, in what I have come to appreciate as Dutch-English, sang a song which I had never heard before:

Because He lives, I can face tomorrow.
   Because He lives, all fear is gone.
Because I know, I know He holds the future;
   And life is worth the living just because He lives.

That did it! The Spirit quickened that reality to me and I was aware of the fellowship of Jesus. Even now the recollection of that experience fills me with great joy.

However, there is a darker side to our fellowship with Jesus. Paul writing to the Christians at Philippi – the tenderest of all his letters – speaks of sharing the sufferings of Christ. Indeed, there can be no resurrection power without sharing Calvary pain. Maybe we do not fully experience the resurrection power of Jesus because we are not dead enough yet to be resurrected. Undoubtedly, in life, the deepest ties of all are forged in human relationships in the dark valleys when the light seems to have faded and sometimes has gone out altogether. So we have the privilege of sharing the sufferings of Christ.

6. Fellowship with God is the final significant occurence of koinonia

This has a deep ethical content. It was St Augustine who said: 'Love God, and do as you like' – but that can never bear the light of the truth of Scripture upon it. The whole emphasis of the Bible is that when I love God, I do as he likes. It is no longer a question of my saying: 'Your wish is my command', but rather looking into the face of God and saying: 'Your command is my wish.'

Fellowship with God is not for those who have chosen to walk in darkness, but for those who want to be separated from the darkness to walk in the light.

There is a depth and wonder about fellowship that we have hardly begun to touch – but many today are dissatisfied with what they have known, and have begun to respond to the Spirit stirring within them to discover what God always intended to be significant relationships within the body of his Son.

Apart from his stay at Ephesus, Paul stayed longer in the city of Corinth than in any other city. Having left Macedonia with his life in danger, he went to Athens where there was little response to his ministry. So he came to Corinth, and remained there for the next eighteen months. Although the events of these months are compressed into a record of seventeen verses in Acts, they were turbulent and difficult until Paul finally moved on to Syria having completed his work in Corinth. During his time in Corinth he formed deep and tender links with the church there – in his letters we see the spiritual shepherd bearing the sorrows and problems of his people on his heart. One of the main areas of his concern was the nature and quality of fellowship within the church. When he was in Ephesus he learned that all was not well in the Corinthian church, so wrote to them giving very constructive teaching about fellowship (1 Cor. 12:12–31).

He lays down four major principles which must govern the Body of Christ if it is ever to function effectively.

1. We all need to assume our responsibilities in the Church

If the foot should say, 'Because I am not a hand I do not belong to the body', it would not for that reason cease to be part of the body. And if the ear should say, 'Because I am not an eye, I do not belong to the body', it would not for that reason cease to be part of the body.

He says quite clearly '. . . in fact God has arranged the parts in the body, every one of them, just as he wanted them to be' and '. . . in the church God has appointed. . .'

In other words, every one of us has been placed in the Body of Christ as God in his sovereign will has desired. We may feel that we or others are in a place of prominence and do not seem to have the right to be there; or that we or others are in a place of obscurity when we feel it should be otherwise. Although this frequently results in frustration, it is not quite the point. The real point is: 'Am I in the place God has put me fulfilling the function God has given me?' To answer that question honestly is to be launched into an anticipation of faith and a peace of heart which is quite incalculable. The first law of spiritual usefulness is that we use what God has given us in the place God has put us; while the second law of usefulness is that we are content with how God is using us and equally content with how others are being used. We all need to accept responsibility for our own task – it is always easier to assume responsibility for someone else's task!

It is comparatively easy to sing Elsie Yale's hymn with

its jolly tune in a singspiration Sunday night round the piano

> 'There's a work for Jesus ready at your hand
> 'Tis a task the Master just for you has planned.
> Haste to do His bidding, yield Him service true;
> There's a work for Jesus none but you can do.'

It is much more difficult to mean it and face the awesome implications of it.

2. We all need to accept our limitations in the Church

If the whole body were an eye, where would be sense of hearing be? If the whole body were an ear, where would be the sense of smell be? But in fact God has arranged the parts in the body, every one of them, just as he wanted them to be.

No one person (or even one group of persons) can function as the whole Body of Christ – no matter how godly or how gifted. Nor does it make any difference whether that person (or group of persons) is paid for his work within the fellowship or not. The implications of this teaching are perfectly clear – the eye has a very limited value when you are holding a conversation on the telephone, and the ear has serious limitations when it comes to threading a needle or eating your dinner.

Sometimes the will of God for an individual within the Body of Christ is to say 'No' – however disappointed others may be; and however misunderstood, misrepresented and criticised he may be. Unhappily, from time to time a person finds himself in a position within the Body of Christ, and the only qualification he has for being there is his inability to say 'No.'

This clear biblical principle frees us from two devastating pressures:

(a) *Fear of other people's criticism*. It is not that others will not criticise us – they will! But we will be liberated from the awful bondage that goes along with it. Long ago John Knox said: 'The voice of our neighbours sounds more loudly in our ears than the voice of God.' It is possible to be so aware and apprehensive about what people are thinking and saying that we are no longer sensitive to the desires of the heart of God. How important it is to know that I am where God wants me to be, although not necessarily where others expect me to be.

(b) *A binding sense of 'oughtness'*. I have constantly struggled with this ever since I became a living member of the Body of Christ. When I am at my desk preparing to teach the Bible, or attending to the necessary administrative and clerical tasks, I feel I 'ought' to be out on the 'patch' visiting homes. When I drive from one home to another, I feel I 'ought' to be back at the desk getting on with what I have left behind and a number of others things which have been set aside for too long. When I am 'on the job', I feel I 'ought' to be home with my family, since I have been out so often and neglected them. I know many will identify with what I have constantly experienced over the years. There is so much to be done; and so much that is worth doing. Often the result is that the most urgent and pressing things get done, while other equally important matters get left aside – and what God wants *me* to do is set aside. It is life lived under the tyranny of the urgent. How easy it is to confirm that the need does not constitute the call – yet how difficult it is to live with the call when the needs are so many.

The only place of peace in the midst of the pain of knowing how disappointed people are in you, whose expectations of you are higher than God's, is confidently to ascertain and have affirmed that you are in the place God wants you to be fulfilling the task he has given you to do.

In the heady days of the Reformation Martin Luther was a well-known protagonist. He was a 'front man' – a bluff and hearty fighter. There was, however, another upon whom Luther depended so much. Philip Melanchthon. Melanchthon was a frail and gentle scholar, so unlike the doughty Luther. One could not have filled the other's role, nor could either have pioneered the Reformation without the other. Together they not only shook the Church, but also Europe and the world. It was in recognising not only their responsibilities, but also their limitations that they functioned so well.

3: We all need to acknowledge others within the Body of Christ

The eye cannot say to the hand 'I don't need you!' And the head cannot say to the feet 'I don't need you!' On the contrary, those parts of the body that seem to be weaker are indispensable, and the parts that we think are less honourable we treat with special honour. . .

Only a deep revolution in our thinking (this can only be in the category of the supernatural and the miraculous) can persuade us that *all* members of the Church are *equally* necessary – the extrovert needs the introvert; the impulsive needs the cautious; the inspirational needs the analytical; the mystical needs the practical; the old need the young; the prominent need the obscure. In Paul's letter to the Corinthian Christians he is quite specific that there are two main destructive factors in fellowship. The first of these is that the superior want to separate from the inferior. The eye feels much more superior to the hand, and the head feels so much more significant than the feet; and so they proudly declare 'I don't need you!' And equally, the inferior want to separate from the superior. The foot feels unimportant and sub-standard when it considers the ability and prominence of the hand and so says 'I do not belong to the body really!' I have found the latter far more of a threat to fellowship than the former in the day to day life of the Fellowship – although neither make pastoring easy!

The other main factor which threatens fellowship is the gifts which we possess. There is the constant tendency to exalt one gift over another and thereby impute to the one who possesses the 'higher' gift a much more important place in the Body of Christ. There has been a lot of talk and teaching these days about gifts in the Body of Christ. Some have even wished that they had never been asked to confront this teaching since it has been disturbing within the Church and the loving atmosphere that once was known has been destroyed. The fault lies, however, not in the discovery of the presence of gifts within the Church, but in the discovery of the absence of love. Perhaps the most serious aspect of this is not that the Church does not have Calvary love, but that she does not have Calvary love although she is convinced she has. It is not without significance that 1 Corinthians 13 is sandwiched between 1 Corinthians 12 and 1 Corinthians 14. The presence and the use of the gifts of God to the Body of Christ can only work effectively when the supernatural love of the cross made real in our hearts by the Holy Spirit is flowing freely within the Fellowship.

4. We all need to appreciate unity in the Church

But God has combined the members of the body and has given greater honour to the parts that lacked it, so that there should be no division in the body, but that its parts should have equal concern for each other. If one part suffers, every part suffers with it; if one part is honoured, every part rejoices with it.

There are many metaphors to describe the Church, but the key to them all is unity. This was the last cry of Jesus to his Father on that last night on earth before his death on the cross. Having prayed for himself and his disciples, he then prayed for us – that we might know unity. Many have taken this heart-cry of Jesus seriously and have concluded that what Jesus really wanted was uniformity. In fact what Jesus is looking for is unanimity – as we proclaim the same message; feel the same love; and know the same power. It is not a visible unity, since Jesus compares it to the unity he has with his Father. It is an invisible resilient reality which is hard to define, but impossible to mistake when it is present. Jesus is not crying to the Father that *we* should accomplish it, but rather that *he* should accomplish it.

There is to be one flock, and one Shepherd; one bride and one Bridegroom; one household and one Father; one vine and one set of branches; one kingdom and one King;

one building and one Cornerstone or Foundation; one body and one Head.

Having discovered this we are to defend it.

So much, then, for the meaning of fellowship and the principles on which it is to function – how can it work in a practical way? The first essential for us in our church was a radical re-appraisal of our traditional structure – especially the structure of our leadership. We had an Eldership, but, although it was warm and godly, it was formal rather than functional. We met one evening each month, but for the practical functioning of fellowship this was totally inadequate. We had House Groups every other Tuesday under the leadership of an elder – but these were something and nothing at the same time. A plurality of leadership, in itself, is not the answer. That leadership has still to develop realistic functioning. Unless it does it can be more of a hindrance than a help. To a lesser degree we continued to struggle with a 'building-centred' concept of Christianity – going to church; being involved in church; still had a strong association with the building where the church here has met over many years.

The elders began to meet weekly, and their area of pastoral responsibility was broken down into much smaller geographical areas within that area. The House Groups were changed to House Fellowships where people who were beginning to grow together were concerned not so much to share their ideas (and their prejudices) as to share their lives. House Fellowship leaders had to be carefully and prayerfully appointed and trained to take over leadership under the guidance of the elder for their area.

So a structure for growth in depth emerged which was confronted with all the inevitable resistance to change. Those of us involved in leadership here constantly need to be sure that God is in this and that changes of this radical nature will benefit not only the church members, but bless God. We began to ask a fundamental question: Why are House Fellowships important and relevant?

We gave seven answers to that question: House Fellowships are important and relevant because:

(a) *There are many needs which can be met there which could never be met in a large meeting of Christians*. For example, it is estimated that anything over 175 people makes interpersonal relationships quite impossible. Dr David Burnett made a study during 1978 of our situation here and made the following comments about it:

> Anonymity of the services – 'I don't know half the people who attend the church', 'Gold Hill is quite big enough for me. I don't know who are the visitors and who have been members several years.' This sort of comment is common. British Churches are usually small having less than 200 members, which means that one can know the names of the people who attend, although not necessarily have close fellowship with all. Visitors can easily be identified. When the church attendance is about 400 one cannot have the same relationship, and individuals can feel lost in the crowd. Other centres of fellowship must be sought therefore, and the house groups should provide this needed dimension. However, this requires a change from the traditional role of the church service, and will not be accepted readily.

Because of the breakdown of interpersonal relationships within the Body of Christ, Christians can often be more intimately and more realistically related to colleagues at work and elsewhere than in the church. This ought not to be so.

Other needs which can be met in House Fellowships are in the areas of practical requirements and individual expression. Caring, cooking, decorating, gardening, transportation, child minding, and other needs can be known and responded to very quickly and with a minimum of organisation. Within the smaller grouping, too, many valuable insights and experiences can helpfully be shared which would never have seen the light of day in a large meeting.

(b) *There is a need for a clear explanation and a confident expression of the gifts of the Father, Son and Holy Spirit*. It is within the security of the House Fellowship that these gifts can be discovered and then developed. This is the place for instruction on their meaning, use and abuse. There is a richness resident within the Body of Christ here which has been damned up for centuries. We need to learn how to release these riches – and in the process be confident enough even to make mistakes. For too long the Church has been dependent on natural gifts dedicated to God – this has led to a mainly middle-class and middle-aged Church. Now, new resources are being recognised and released to the glory of God which have nothing to do with human ability or length of experience.

(c) *There is a need to reach out significantly into the community*. The church building was never meant to be the place for significant Christian outreach. The intention of Jesus is that we should be out where the people are. Jesus' instructions were in the first instance to 'go and tell' before he gave the invitation to 'come and see'.

There is so much that is strange in a church building for the uninitiated – often the uncomfortable seats; bewilderment at where to sit; the strange behaviour of standing to sing and refraining from smoking although there are no notices to tell you so; the Victorian language; the Norman architecture and the Roman dress all add up to this strangeness. It is all very bewildering. I remember a vicar's wife from the East End of London telling me that she had deliberately gone to a Bingo Cinema once to get a flavour of what it must be like to go into totally unfamiliar surroundings – should she pay at the door? could she sit anywhere? was it a distraction to talk to her neighbour? once the 'eyes down' was given when could she look up again? – and so on. These difficulties of the unfamiliar and the unusual are not so overwhelming in an ordinary home. There is a degree of normality there and a greater possibility of scratching people where they itch instead of solving problems few are facing and answering questions which no one is asking.

(d) *There is a need for effective oversight*. How can you ever know that each member of the body is rightly related to the head if you are not even sure where they live or have difficulty remembering the names of their children, and are quite clueless about what stage these children are at at school or college?

If each member is to be in the place God has put it, fulfilling the task God has given it, then clear objective guidance has to be given and significant confirmation and accountability needs to be undertaken.

The ministries that Christ has given to his Church are there to secure right relationships among the members so that all will function in an effective and creative way. On any battlefield it is never contemplated that everyone will do his own thing as and when he has the opportunity. In the heat of the battle the followers need to know who the leaders are and have confidence in them to secure the victory; and the leaders need to know who and where the followers are and to trust them to play their significant part.

The pressing question in Christian leadership is not; 'Is it valid?' but 'Is it effective?'

(e) *There is a need for flexibility to replace rigidity*. During the course of my years in the ministry, I have watched the simplest decisions and tasks take an agonisingly long time to be dealt with by the whole church – although seldom was the whole church involved anyway in decision making. Once we wanted to move the Sunday School from after the Morning Service to before the Morning Service. On the face of it a comparatively easy move to achieve. But not so! Months ensued of discussion and debate over the pros and cons; the principles involved and the practical implications. In the end we did what we set out to do – although not everyone was satisfied anyway! Much easier to handle the timing of events, the change of location, the programme which will be provided, and so on within the intimacy of the House Fellowship. Sometimes the work of God has remained static because some of us could not bring ourselves to face up to the hassle and difficulties involved in the mechanics of making that change. The result has been a rigidity which has grown up and stifled the life of some venture of faith. It is often much later that we wake up to discover that God has moved on somewhere else while we have gone on playing our spiritual games. God loves to do the same thing differently. Sometimes, because of our rig-idity, what we are doing is frankly boring. The plea that I am making here is not for novelty, but for flexibility.

(f) *There is a need to make provision for an emergency alternative*. The thing I have in mind could cover a wide spectrum – from the simplest and most straightforward problem such as damage to a part or the whole of the church building to persecution of the Christian Church from within our society. Some of the things which my parents declared would never happen in our country are now, if not daily, certainly regular occurences portrayed vividly on the media. Who can tell what the future holds for the Church of the living God within our society – par-ticularly as that Giant is stirring and will move forward in power making his presence felt in establishing the Kingdom of God among men. Often our security has been the measure of our spiritual and practical poverty.

On my desk this morning I have a magazine with a magnificent photograph of Canterbury Cathedral on the cover. Inside it explains: Cover photograph – Canterbury Cathedral, the Mother Church of the Anglican Com-munion. I find Canterbury Cathedral awe-inspiring and to walk and worship within it deeply moving. For me it was an unforgettable experience – and yet the Church, Anglican or otherwise, is never a building. It is people – ordinary people, redeemed by the grace of God through the death and resurrection of our Lord Jesus Christ, and filled with the Holy Spirit, enabling them to become partakers of the life of God.

With or without a recognisable building, the Church should be recognisable. The presence or absence of an 'official' church building should not affect the mission and ministry of the Church. There were no church buildings during the first 300 years of the Church's life – and these were halcyon days of growth and development.

(g) *There is a need for loving and effective correction*. Be-cause of the public and 'official' nature of discipline, often we have only paid lip-service to it. We have agreed in principle that correction is biblical and necessary, and we write it into our books of rules, yet we hesitate to implement it because the climate is so formal and can make discipline distasteful and destructive.

I have found that those in whom the Lord's life has been born are eager to know that what they are doing is right and pleasing to him, and are anxious to know if they are doing wrong. It is not only unhelpful, but frankly unloving to allow someone to go on without either the confirmation of the right or the correction of the wrong.

The House Fellowship provides the necessary climate of loving and caring which make correction, if not easy, certainly natural and effective.

Dr Griffith Evans of the Medical Research Council in England conducted experiments for twenty-five years with honeymoon couples to ascertain the nature of and the treatment for the common cold. He injected each of these couples with a virus of the common cold. But never once, in a quarter of a century of these experiments, did any of these honeymoon couples catch a cold! Dr Evans came to the conclusion that where there is real love and joy in the system, this will protect the person against disease. Who can tell the implications of the Body of Christ functioning properly in all its different parts as it is related supernaturally in the power of the Holy Spirit, not only to resist infection, but also to be mightily effective.

7: The gifts of the Holy Spirit
– the giant's father gives good gifts to him

'Are you a charismatic then?' After all these years the question still startles me. Normally it follows some comment I have made; or some conviction I have stated; or even some experience I have recalled. I think my reaction is determined by the tone of voice in which the question is asked. Often the tone expresses the same concern as: 'Are you a diabetic then?' or 'Are you an alcoholic then?' However, with diabetes or alcoholism you can be reasonably sure of the symptoms – the former has something to do with the sugar level in the body, while the latter has to do with an uncontrollable drink problem. The symptoms of the charismatic are never quite so straightforward. The 'Are you a Charismatic then?' question can mean anything from 'Do you really swing from the chandeliers?' or 'Do you jig from foot to foot waving your hands around in the air and call it dancing before the Lord?' or 'Do you speak in tongues?' or 'Are you prepared to receive everything that God wants to give you to equip you to serve him – even if it is not in your tradition and is liable to be misunderstood?'

The basic and most general reality which lies behind the so-called 'Charismatic Movement' is that God is a Father who loves to give good gifts to his children.

When we come to the end of our hoarded resources,
Our Father's full-giving has only begun.
His love has no limit, His grace has no measure,

His power no boundary known unto men.
For out of His infinite riches in Jesus,
He giveth, and giveth, and giveth again.

It is one of the characteristics of fatherhood that he gives
to his children – and his children expect him to! On the
day of Pentecost the over-all gift of the Holy Spirit came to
those who were in the right place in obedience to the directions of the risen Christ and in the right attitude of
fellowship with one another. One particular gift was man-
ifested straight away and then another, and then another.
God began to give these particular Gifts to his people so
that they would have the ability to do something for others
which would strengthen and build up the Body of Christ.
The Puritan theologian John Owen says: 'Gifts proceed
solely from the regal office and power of Christ. They are
all given unto and distributed for the good of the Church,
but they are effects only of His kingly power.' That many
emotionally balanced, theologically aware, earnest, God-
honouring, Christ-centred Christians within the framework
of the historical church as well as in Pentecostal churches
have experienced and expressed the gifts of the Holy Spirit
in recent years cannot be doubted. Have they been deluded
or are they self-deceived? Many replies are given, but three
main views are held.

The first of these is that the gifts of the Holy Spirit were
given to the early Church to 'get it going'. The particular
need of the early Church which these gifts supplied was
teaching, guidance and instruction since the New Testament had not yet been written. Generally, this view explains, the Church needed supernatural authentication of
its life. However, with regard to the particular need, it
would seem that these early disciples had even more (in the
sense of depth and reality) instruction than we have. The
'Acts' Church apparently 'devoted themselves to the apostles' teaching' on a very regular – perhaps even daily –
basis. They were much closer to the earthly life of Christ
than we are, and Paul can quote the words of Jesus to the
Elders at Ephesus, 'It is more blessed to give than to re-

ceive' even though they are not recorded in the Gospels, and expect their recognition of them. Presumably the instruction now within the New Testament was being used in the Church throughout this period even though it was not committed to writing until towards the end of the first century. With regard to the general need of the Church, not only does every 'generation need regeneration', but that regeneration needs authentication. The Church on earth is never a permanent structure, but a living, growing, developing organism, part of which is constantly being promoted to become part of the Church triumphant in heaven, and part of which is as new as a new-born baby on earth. If the gifts of the Holy Spirit were necessary during the morning glory of the Church, how much more are they required today.

The second view holds that though the gifts of the Holy Spirit were not permanently withdrawn, they emerge only at the discretion of the Spirit himself. So they will appear and disappear from age to age. Their absence or presence is the sole responsibility of the Holy Spirit. There is a divine unpredictability about them. Charles Simeon held this view. He says: 'I think then, we may say, that learning must supply the place of miracles, unless God should be pleased to restore to his Church those powers which for so many centuries have been withdrawn.' Although the passage has controversial manuscript evidence, Mark at the end of his gospel records the words of Jesus 'and these signs will accompany those who believe'. This is as authentic in Mark's Gospel as the great commission of Jesus to 'Go into all the world and preach the Good News to all creation.'

If we take one pronouncement of Jesus as authentic, may we not logically, and as a matter of integrity, take the other. Again, Paul instructs us to 'eagerly desire the greater gifts' in the context of the gifts of the Holy Spirit. It is not an encouragement, within this context, as some have supposed, to choose the way of love rather than the way of gifts. He says quite specifically that it is not either love or gifts we are to be concerned over, but both love and gifts. 'Follow the way of love' he says, 'and eagerly desire spiritual gifts, especially the gifts of prophecy.' In view of this, inevitably this second view embraces a doctrine of frustration. According to its conclusion, the Bible encourages us to desire something which can never be satisfied because the Spirit has withdrawn the gifts. This runs counter to all that Scripture teaches us about the heart and purposes of God. God never puts hungers within us which have no hope of ever being satisfied.

Both these views tend to give an explanation for the absence of the gifts of the Holy Spirit both individually and corporately, and do little to explain their presence.

The third view unreservedly acknowledges that the gifts of the Holy Spirit have been given by God to the Church to enable her to live the Jesus-life in every generation until the next great historical event occurs – the return of our Lord Jesus Christ. Looking at the Bible as a whole, there is a marked absence of any statement in the New Testament which would lead us to believe that either Christ or the apostles regarded the gifts of the Holy Spirit as temporary. The only passage which deals with this in fact teaches the exact opposite. In that great chapter, 1 Corinthians 13, Paul is contrasting the graces – faith, hope and love – with the gifts. He is saying that while these graces are permanent, the gifts will 'cease . . . be stilled' and so are temporary. The question is – when will this happen? Happily Paul tells us – 'when perfection comes'. Most commentators are agreed that this is a reference to the return of our Lord Jesus Christ. These gifts will then be withdrawn because they will no longer be necessary. He will reign supremely and we will be like him.

Writing about the Montanists John Wesley said: 'The grand reason why the miraculous gifts were so soon withdrawn was not only that faith and holiness were well-nigh lost; but that dry, formal, orthodox men began even then to ridicule whatever gifts they had not themselves; and to decry them all, as either madness or imposture.' We need to heed the warning lest we excuse our spiritual condition with theological gymnastics.

There are two words commonly used in speaking of the

103

gifts – one is *charisma* (plural = *charismata*) and means the evidence of the sheer undeserved generosity of the heart of God; the other is *phaneros* which means God sharing himself as he is. The word 'gift' is itself a good word, since it reminds us that these blessings cannot be earned or deserved, but are freely given by God to his children. A gift is not normally a reward for good behaviour or fine achievement (that is either a prize or a bribe), but a sign of a real relationship.

There are two questions which we need to ask about the gifts of the Holy Spirit.

1. What are they for?
2. What are they?

Let's take the first question and answer it: 'What are these gifts for?'

There has been an unhappy contrasting and assumed conflict between the gifts of the Holy Spirit and the fruit of the Holy Spirit. The gifts of the Holy Spirit are given to enable us to manifest the *conduct* of Christ, whereas the fruit of the Holy Spirit is formed by the Holy Spirit to enable us to manifest the *character* of Christ. Jesus did not only say to the sick and the crippled who came to him: 'I love you.' He said: 'Be healed.' One of the saddest and most frustrating things in human experience is loving people and yet not being able to do very much to help them. Both the gifts and the fruit are important. The love of Jesus was always backed by his power and the power of Jesus was always tempered by his love. But both were present and active as he ministered within the world. The gifts of the Spirit are not badges to be worn or trophies to be displayed; they are tools to be used by good, honest workmen, who know the life and calling of God to manifest the life of Jesus on earth. They are the means whereby divine grace will become tangible and visible among men and women.

The fruit of the Holy Spirit (love, joy, peace, patience, gentleness, kindness, faith, humility and discipline) is to be formed in each member of the Body of Christ – one fruit with nine flavours! These nine flavours are to be seen and identified within each individual. The gifts of the Holy Spirit are, however, spread among the members of the Body of Christ – so that anyone may have one or more gifts, but none will ever possess all of the gifts.

There are two quite deep practical misunderstandings which constantly impede the progress and development of the Giant – the sub-conscious belief that the Church is a building, and the restriction of relevant ministry to a comparative few within it. The gifts of the Spirit are given by God to enable the members of the Body of Christ to function properly and fully as he intended. They have nothing whatever to do with status, but everything to do with functioning. Lewis Pethrus has written in his book *The Wind Bloweth Where It Listeth*, 'There are some who say they have gifts of the Spirit, but who never want to use them in church. Why is it easier to bring forth the gifts in a little cottage prayer meeting? They feel hesitant of the fiery test to which messages are put in the full assembly of God's people.' Difficulties arise, of course, when a church is spiritually dead and doctrinally bankrupt. That difficulty does not cancel out, however, the fact that these gifts were and are given to make the Body of Christ relevant in manifesting the life of Jesus.

Again, the gifts of the Holy Spirit are given by God to enable the active participation of *all* the members of the Body of Christ. Christians do not follow signs, but signs follow Christians. There needs to be a supernatural, visible show from each one without exception which can only be explained in terms of God. Dr Emil Brunner in '*The Misunderstanding of the Church*' writes:

> One thing is extremely important; that *all* minister, and that nowhere is to be perceived a separation or even merely a distinction between those who do, and those who do not minister, between the active and the passive members of the Body of Christ, between those who give and those who receive. There exists in the *ekklesia* a universal duty and right of service, a universal readiness

to serve, and at the same time the greatest possible differentiation of function.

Michael Green emphasises the same thing in his book *Called to Serve*.

> If we were to ask the New Testament writers, 'What is the difference between a clergyman and layman?' they would not understand what we meant. For the Christianity of the New Testament does not know two classes of Christian, the professional and the amateur, so to speak. All Christians are the *laity* of God (1 Pet. 1:10 – Greek: *laos*). All Christians, likewise, are ministers of God. . . The New Testament knows nothing of a priestly caste.

We are constantly confronted within the Church by two dangers with regard to the gifts of the Holy Spirit. The first of these is that we equate these gifts, both in their nature and the number of them possessed by any one person, with the amount of love God has for that person. This is, of course, how we normally think from a human point of view – the greater the number of gifts I give to someone indicates the level of love I have for him. While this is neither true socially nor spiritually, that sub-conscious conclusion remains. Instead, we need to equate the gifts God has given with the purpose God has for that person. The second danger is that we can be persuaded that any gift we may possess is important on its own. It never is. It will only find its importance in relation to the Body of Christ.

It is one thing to believe that the gifts of the Holy Spirit are for today and that God gives them to strengthen and equip the Body of Christ for the work of serving now; it is quite another to begin to 'let it happen' in a practical way in a local church situation. I remember years ago a visitor who had been an overseas missionary and had been 'sent home' from the mission field because of his charismatic activity came to live in our area. He soon gathered a group of people around him on a weekly basis to teach them charismatic things. The largest percentage of that group came from our church. I had a great concern about it, but, in those days, felt quite powerless to alter the situation. The day came, however, when the visitor quite suddenly and very unexpectedly left the area. The group was left leaderless and those who belonged to our church asked if I would meet with them. I did! Their concern was two-fold – that I should continue to teach them from where our visitor had left them, and that they should continue to meet as a group in order 'to manifest the gifts of the Holy Spirit'. I refused! I could not continue from where the visitor had left off since I did not know where he had been, where he was, or where he was going to in his teaching. In any case, I had been called to pastor the local church, and not a tiny segment within it.

With regard to the second concern, I felt strongly that such a group, meeting 'to manifest the gifts of the Holy Spirit', was unhealthy, unproductive and divisive. When I met with them I indicated that this was the first and the last time that we would meet as a group – and we all went home! I gave strong encouragement, however, to the group to become more actively involved in the full life of the church with the absolute assurance that as long as I was in leadership there would be opportunity to express the gifts of the Holy Spirit as and when the Lord required. In hindsight I am amazed that such counselling and guidance came from me since I was so inexperienced and insecure personally in the whole area. I am sure, beyond any personal doubt, that my leadership in this matter was right, but I am equally sure that the source of my leadership came directly from God. In retrospect, too, I am sure that the encouragement to have freedom to express the gifts of the Spirit in the normal life of the church was a direct act of faith since there were few around in those days in a local church situation who could offer any practical help. Although I had an inkling, little did I know how strong ecclesiastical tradition and theological prejudice could be when convictions from the Bible came to be implemented in practice. God was so gracious in those early days in that the emergence of spiritual gifts was slow and gentle.

The elders of our church felt it right that I should begin to give specific, consecutive Bible teaching to the whole church on the person and ministry of the Holy Spirit. We devoted a great deal of time to this. So much so that there were those who felt and said that as a church we had become Holy Spirit-centred rather than Christ-centred. That was not true, nor is it true today. I remember many weeks during which in the morning Bible Study on a Sunday I taught on each gift of the Holy Spirit in 1 Corinthians 12. In the evening of each of these Sundays we met in the church hall after the evening service to talk together about the morning teaching (these were days before the House Fellowships had really come into their own). I recall two impressions of these Sunday evenings – one of great personal apprehension (if not terror!) about my ability to handle the questions, comments and criticism; the other of a gentle, gracious warmth and understanding in the congregation that we were all in this together and there did not seem to be any 'experts' around. These were not easy days, but they were good days when, unknown to most of us, we were laying down foundations upon which God would be able to build. The more recognisable gifts of the Spirit form a part of our normal life together now – and we are all the better for believing that God is much more patient with us than we are with one another.

The other question which we need to ask about the gifts (*charismata*) of the Holy Spirit is: 'What are they?'

Inherent in the word *charismata* is the Greek word *charis* which is normally translated 'grace'. With this Paul begins and ends each of his letters which have been included in the New Testament. For Paul, 'grace' alone explains the heights and depths of his own religious experience. He knew what he had been, and he knew what he was – and there was no possible explanation of the change other than the grace of God. For him, 'grace' was central because he could never forget what grace had done for him, and daily he was seeing what grace could do for all men who would receive it. Dr James Moffatt once said: 'Grace needs no supplement.' It is the very essence of the Christian Gospel.

Dr Moffatt, in his book *Grace in the New Testament*, says that Paul's faith and religion can be summed up in one brief sentence: 'All is of grace, and grace is for all.' So *charis*; *charisma*; *charismata* form a very lovely group of words. They declare two things about God.

(a) *They declare God's Beauty. Charis* is a lovely thing. It can speak of physical beauty and charm. It always moves in the realm of winsomeness, loveliness and attractiveness. There are some Christian terms which have within them the atmosphere of sternness and severity. But grace, in the Christian sense, is a thing of such surpassing beauty that the heart bows down in wondering adoration before it.

(b) *They declare God's Bounty. Charis* always has within it the idea of a gift which is completely free and entirely undeserved. The ideas of grace and merit are mutually exclusive, and entirely contradictory. To put grace and merit together would be like talking about a black snowball.

No one can earn grace. It can only be humbly, gratefully and adoringly received. The fundamental idea of grace is a gift given out of the generosity of the giver's heart.

Where a *charisma* (gift) or *charismata* (gifts) of the Holy Spirit are being expressed it is an evidence of God at work in his beauty and his bounty. The goal of the gifts of the Holy Spirit is not simply that something actually happens, but that glory is brought to God.

Someone has said that 'if the Holy Spirit were to withdraw from his Church 97 per cent of the activities would probably continue without missing a step.' We would still speak audibly with our eyes closed and call it prayer; stand to sing our hymns with our minds miles away and call it praise and worship; preach our sermons thoughtfully, eloquently, and with theological accuracy, expecting nothing to happen and call it co-operating with God; organise our programme with no anticipation of God moving unmistakably and dramatically and call it the plan of God. It really is not a question of 'do I like it?' but rather, 'Is this true?' Sadly, we have allowed this glorious organism, which was meant to be the channel of the grace of God and a manifestation of the life of Christ, to become a mere human institution on a par with other good human institutions and at the mercy of the good ideas of men. What is there to distinguish the Church from a good Rotary Club or a good Women's Rural Institute?

The gifts of the Holy Spirit have been given by God, not in response to man's ability, holiness or maturity, but as the result of his grace being released among his people. We have turned to 1 Corinthians 12 to identify the gifts of the Holy Spirit – and this is right. But it is sad that we have come to speak and to think of the gifts (*charismata*) in terms only of the nine gifts which are listed there. Sometimes when none of these nine gifts is expressed in the public congregation there is often disappointment and people say: 'The Spirit did not do anything today!' While all of these nine gifts are valid and available today, yet they are only samples of what God wants to do so that we know 'God is here'.

The nine gifts of the Holy Spirit in 1 Corinthians 12 can be divided into three groups:

1. POWER TO KNOW
   - the message of wisdom
   - the message of knowledge
   - the ability to distinguish between spirits.

2. POWER TO SAY
   - prophecy
   - the ability to speak in different kinds of tongues
   - the interpretation of tongues.

3. POWER TO DO
   - faith
   - gifts of healing
   - miraculous powers

The Bible itself, however, widens the concept of *charismata*. It speaks of fellowship, justification, eternal life, serving, teaching, exhortation, contributing, administrating the Church, doing acts of mercy, singleness, deliverance from deadly perils, pastoring as *charisma* or *charismata*. This in no way devalues the gifts of the Holy Spirit by demoting them to the commonplace and the ordinary. Quite the reverse occurs – instead of lowering the *charismata* to the level of the ordinary and the natural, it raises the ordinary and the commonplace into the level of the extraordinary and the supernatural. God is not calling us to an occasional experience of one of the nine charismatic gifts, but he wants us to express a charismatic life – a life which ultimately can only be explained in terms of God.

We are so prone to divide life into self-contained compartments. We say: 'That is religious or sacred and that is secular; that is natural and this is supernatural.' For example, praying, reading the Bible, attending church, giving an offering are sacred activities, while going to work, driving the car, washing the dishes, doing the shopping, are secular activities. God makes no such distinction. He wants his life to break forth as clearly when I am washing the dishes as when I am preaching a sermon. We often speak of prophesying, speaking in tongues, healing the sick, discerning spirits, as supernatural or charismatic, whereas singing hymns, giving an offering, playing the organ in a church service, encouraging a friend, is natural. The New Testament makes it quite clear that any of these activities could be religious or secular, either supernatural or natural. The determining factor does not lie in the nature of the activity itself, but in the motivation (why am I doing this?) behind it, and in the source (how is it possible for me to manifest Jesus' life through this?) of its power. No matter what we do, however *good* its appearance, can be either *natural* (i.e. designed and energised by the flesh) or *charismatic* (i.e. designed and energised by the Holy Spirit). Religious work can be done well and skilfully without spiritual gifts, but work designed for and which will endure for eternity calls for the functioning of the Holy Spirit through the gifts which he imparts. In other words, the gifts of the Holy Spirit need to become part of everyday life. The great danger of the twentieth century evidences of the Holy Spirit is that we 'domesticate' him – we keep him within the confines of the household of faith. He came to enable us to demonstrate the robust and resilient reality of the Jesus life wherever we are and whatever we are doing.

You show me a church where the gifts of the Holy Spirit

are operating with love and I will show you a church where God is moving mightily and the Gospel of Christ is being allowed to penetrate society in a relevant, life-changing way.

It might well be asked: 'Why have these gifts been disregarded, criticised or neglected for so long?' There are two main reasons for this. The *first* is that in the West there has been and there continues to be an unbalanced emphasis on the intellect and the ability of human reason. Consequently, little room is left for more direct inspiration. If I cannot understand and grasp something, then I need not believe it since it is unlikely to be true. Such has been the conclusion many of us have arrived at. As communications have improved, however, we have become more and more aware of a cleavage which has existed for such a long time between the Eastern and Western Churches. Those in the East have allowed much more scope for the Holy Spirit and his more direct ways of inspiration, whereas those in the West have emphasised reason and logic. Only our Western pride would enable us to presume that the latter is much more realistic than the former. The *second* is that excess and fanaticism has often accompanied the gifts of the Holy Spirit. The Church has always been in difficulty over exercising godly discipline even when it has been able to distinguish between the true and the false. If you cannot distinguish between the flesh and the Spirit, the bogus and the authentic, and if you cannot exercise a proper control when you do, it is inevitable that prohibition will result. Irenaeus, writing at the end of the second century, describes those who 'mock the gifts of the Spirit'. He goes on to say: 'It is with them as with others, in order to get rid of false brethren they deny the whole brotherhood.'

Jonathan Edwards, in the eighteenth century, defends the revival which had taken place in New England by saying to its critics that they were showing the human weakness of 'either approving or condemning all in a lump'. This is the easy way to deal with a problem – although never the most fruitful or satisfactory! God has called us to exercise sober judgment and so distinguish carefully between what is of man and what is of God. Where control is exercised; biblical principles laid down clearly and observed; the honour and glory of God lovingly and primarily sought, the 'new' movement of the Holy Spirit accompanied by the gifts which he so graciously gives is not only healthy, but is indispensable for the accomplishing of our very reason for being alive.

Let Jonathan Edwards have the final word. To him the revival in his day was a glorious work of God. His critics thought otherwise and suggested that it displayed symptoms of insanity in those involved. Edward's rejoinder was terse and to the point: 'Now if such things are enthusiasm and the fruits of distempered brain, let my brain be evermore possessed of that happy distemper!'

8: Leadership and authority

Whenever God does a work among his people, he raises up leadership, sometimes to inititate his work, but always to oversee and further it. Perhaps no other area stirs such deep emotions; engenders more apprehension, if not fear; and causes such deep conflict than this. Often when we desire leadership ourselves, or discredit the leaders who are set in authority over us, even where there is integrity and godliness, we do not fully realise the magnitude of their task. We are prone to observe only the observable and be unaware of the hidden battles of the soul; the conflict which is incessant with the powers of darkness; the unspectacular and yet enormously demanding unseen ministries that make public leadership a possibility.

I was many years in the ministry before I fully realised that God had not called me simply to do as well as and if possible better than what others had done in generations past, but to lead the people of God forward to another stage in building 'the Kingdom of God on earth as it is in heaven'. I discovered quickly what a congregation expected of me – to preach regularly three times a week throughout the year; to be as diligent in visitation as my predecessor, only more so; to take responsibility for chairmanship of church organised gatherings; to represent the church in a variety of ways locally and elsewhere; and to foster the traditions which had grown up round the truth and formed a comfortable and often predictable context in which to operate. This kind of job description – expected though not expressed – although daunting, was not unattractive to me. I revelled in it (apart from the 'chairing' bit!). I was absorbed, but I was lonely. Ultimately I became dissatisfied, not with the job, but with myself, for those I worked with and amongst were the dearest and most gracious and generous people I had met. I sensed that there must be more to being a Christian than I had so far discovered. I determined to explore spiritual geography and then lead others into these discoveries. Someone has said 'it is not difficult to be a Christian – it is impossible!' At this stage, although demanding, I was still in the dimension of the possible, even if it meant sacrificing my personal and family life in the process.

When God called Moses to lead his people out of slavery into what he had planned for them, it was an impossible task. A military strategist has catalogued the immensity of the task. He has pointed out:

1. There was a minimum of two million people who had to be got out of Egypt. Quite a task when you consider the difficulty involved in securing political asylum for one person today.
2. Egypt was the most fortified country then known. It was bounded on its western side by desert and on its eastern side by a line of fortresses which were designed not only to keep an aggressor out, but also to keep the population (both willing and unwilling) in. To the south it was bounded by the Red Sea. Egypt had an understanding with neighbouring territories that any fugitives from her should be returned.
3. The route to be taken by the people of God under Moses leadership was via one of the most desolate deserts in the world, where many have subsequently perished even in recent years.
4. Nine hundred tons of food would be required to sustain the humans and livestock each day.
5. Two thousand four hundred tons of firewood would be required for cooking – and that in a scrubby desert!
6. Two million gallons of water would be needed to slake the thirst of both animals and men – and that in a desert which had become so through lack of water!

Surely, too, there was little psychological or emotional encouragement for Moses – Genesis had begun in perfection (God looked at what he had created and was very pleased with what he saw), but ended in death (the last word in the book of Genesis is 'coffin').

Such was the task of leadership given to Moses. It is one thing reflecting on what I might be able to do or recognising what God's people might want me to do – it is quite another responding to what God has planned in his time that I should be part of. I do not think I was sufficiently aware in these early years of what God was looking for in his leaders. I think my ignorance was encouraged by my own personal selection for the task of being a pastor. The local church where I had been reared did not select me – indeed they knew little, if anything, about God's calling on my life. Their guidance, support, and confirmation was never asked for nor did I know that I could ever expect to receive it. It seemed to me that the most important question that had to be answered was; 'Could I preach?' My father, probably, would have been the best judge of this since he regularly listened to me as a teenager on a Saturday evening as we toured the Gospel tea-meetings within a radius of about twenty miles of my home town. These would be the equivalent spiritually of the working men's clubs in the industrial areas of the country today. We were a kind of Gospel concert party – not very original or competent, but certainly very sincere. The smell of stewing tea, freshly baked cakes on a baker's board, and an overheated building with condensation running down the windows still evokes a certain nostalgia within me. But as far as the church was concerned I was asked to speak at the mid-week prayer meeting in my own church, and subsequently to preach at the morning service in a neighbouring church about ten miles away – and on the recommendation of these two pastors I was considered suitable material for training in Christian leadership. The church was quite clearly the handmaid of the college I attended and not vice versa. This was not surprising in view of the poverty of the church. I can remember great emphasis being placed on academic training, and it seemed likely that this Christian leader might well be frustrated through lack of understanding of the Greek language (for some reason Hebrew did not seem to be quite so important). It is not that I am complaining about the need for theological training – indeed I warmly commend it, and the Church will always be the poorer without it. I came to realise years later that what God was looking for was someone who had heard his call to be his leader whatever the consequence to personal ambition, future security and social esteem, and who was prepared to be nothing in order that he might be everything. I have come to see in more recent years that only those who are totally available to the church (and so often totally supported by the church) will have the most significant leadership impact within the church. Significantly, the company upon whom the Spirit of God fell on the day of Pentecost numbered 120, and, of these, twelve were totally available to it. Wherever such leadership is discovered, God is prepared to do a mighty work. God will work on those whom he has in mind until he achieves what he is looking for. It took God a long time to fashion Moses. For forty years Moses was trained in how to be a somebody in Egypt. For the next forty years he was trained in how to be a nobody in the desert. At the age of eighty God began to show Moses – and the world – what he can do with a nobody. I remember being deeply impressed with Moses' arguments with God against his suitability for leadership of his people, having spent forty years minding sheep. He seemed to be saying: 'There was a day when it might have been possible – I spoke the same language of the Egyptians; I understood their ways; I had a certain authority among them; I was more able and equipped intellectually than most of them. But look at me now with my weatherbeaten features, my calloused hands, my peasant's clothes, my coarse speech that has an impediment anyway, and shepherds are denigrated by the Egyptians' (Gen. 46:34). At a missionary weekend I once heard Henry Guinness (OMF) say of Hudson Taylor (the founder of CIM/OMF) that he was a man 'small enough for God to use'. It really is not a question of age, ability, or possessions that makes a leader, but it is a question of attitude.

Again we need to be aware that we are involved in spiritual warfare. Ever since Satan rebelled, he has sought to smuggle the sins of independence, disobedience, and rebellion into the Church of the living God, and these are still prevalent dangers today. To use words like authority or submission is to create anxiety if not resistance. Satan thrives on our apprehensiveness of leadership and authority in a biblical sense since he knows that no army can be effective in real warfare if there is no clear leadership and no distinguishable commitment from the followers. On the battlefield defeat is assured when everyone does what is right 'in his own eyes'. But clearly God has called us not just to be sons and servants, but also to be soldiers waging war at close quarters with the power of darkness. Dr Martyn Lloyd-Jones once said that Christianity is far too often presented as a remedy that you need to help you with your problems.' But, comments Dr Lloyd-Jones: 'In the Bible I find a barracks, not a hospital. It is not a doctor you need, but a Sergeant-Major. Here we are on the parade ground slouching about. A doctor is no good; it is discipline we need. We need to listen to the Sergeant-Major – "yield not to temptation, but yield yourselves to God." This is the trouble with the Church today; there is too much of the hospital element; they have lost sight of the great battle.' Significantly, much of the Old Testament is devoted to the wars of Israel – to teach us how to fight the good fight of faith. In the New Testament the whole concept of Christ's Kingdom coming upon men is presented in terms of military invasion. In the New Testament letters there are continual references to spiritual warfare. Many have wanted Christian blessings without Christian battles only to discover that God has called us not only to a Christian walk, but also to Christian warfare.

As the Sleeping Giant stirs the warfare inevitably intensifies because the Kingdom of Darkness is threatened and will fight back with cunning as well as with strength. The need to recognise and respond to godly leadership becomes of paramount importance.

As more and more people live on earth, the question 'What is the ideal form of government?' becomes more and more urgent. How is it possible to maintain law and liberty in perfect balance? How can you keep affairs under control and yet ensure freedom and give opportunity for individual enterprise?

The government of the world at the moment is roughly divided into two main expressions – democracy and dictatorship. In a democracy every person has a right to a voice in government. The people have the ability and the authority to choose and to change the government when and if they feel it is right to do so. There are two difficulties, however, as far as we are concerned as Christians with democracy. The first is that in the late twentieth century democracy is shaking. This is the inevitable result of the outworking of human nature. Human nature is sinful, and so my rights will eventually overtake my responsibilities. Sooner or later there is a conflict of personal interests and the result is a downward spiral of selfishness, violence and anarchy. When I demand my rights I step out of God's will; when I take my responsibilities seriously I step into God's will. The second difficulty with democracy is that it is not a biblical concept. It springs from the pagan thinking of Plato in the fifth century BC. It is in fact not the will of God that everybody should run everything. This is a godless concept which has found acceptance by man – even within the church. The priesthood of all believers is there in the Bible to encourage personal devotion not to explain corporate democracy.

In a dictatorship the people are not free to choose. Dictatorship says 'no' to democracy and imposes its rule upon people. History, of course, has demonstrated some of the grave weaknesses of dictatorship. There is a great fear – and it is not unfounded – that the alternative to democracy is dictatorship. If that is so politically, it is not so spiritually. Neither dictatorship nor democracy is owned by God.

God's plan for government is theocracy – government by

God himself. In practical terms, God's government is exercised through some being responsible for the leadership of others, and both being responsible to Jesus Christ. This is neither democracy nor dictatorship. Leadership is God's gift to the Church and he has the responsibility for appointing it and it is solemnly accountable to him. Carnality, a lack of appreciation of the person and the true ministry of the Holy Spirit, and the elevation of human expediency over divine principle has substituted man's ways for God's in the running of God's affairs in terms of the choice and functioning of leadership within the Body of Christ, and the Kingdom of God has been impoverished as a result.

There are three words used for church leaders in the Bible; they can be translated in five ways, but they define one function – *leadership*.

1. *Episkopos* = 'a bishop' or 'an overseer'. This refers to the position of spiritual authority which the leader occupies.

2. *Presbuteros* = 'an elder'. This refers to the leader being a person of spiritual maturity.

3. *Poimēn* – 'a shepherd' or 'a pastor'. This refers to God's purpose for his leaders in exercising spiritual responsibility.

By definition a *leader* is a person of spiritual maturity accepting spiritual responsibility before the Lord and exercising spiritual authority. Incidentally, the names are interchangeable – the bishop is an elder; the elder is a pastor; and the pastor is a bishop (cf. Acts 20; Titus 1:5–7; 1 Pet. 5).

We need to examine these offices within the Church much more closely.

1. Episkopos

The word comes from two Greek words which literally mean 'to watch over' or 'to see over'. Etymologically it always carries with it a note of authority. In classical Greek it was used of the gods as well as men to describe their function. In secular society it was frequently used of magistrates (they, incidentally, sometime administered finances in the heathen Temples). In the New Testament it is used of Christ (1 Pet. 2:25), of apostles (Acts 1:20), and of leaders in the local church.

2. Presbuteros

This is the most frequently used word for leaders in the Church. The significance of elders can scarcely be exaggerated. Indeed, it would seem that a group of believers without scriptural leadership will never constitute a New Testament church. For example, in Acts 14:21–3 there is a transition which takes place between verses 22 and 23. In v. 22 believers are referred to as disciples, but in v. 23 elders are ordained and the concept of church is introduced. Groups of disciples became churches when scriptural leadership was appointed. Again in Titus 1:5 'The reason I left you in Crete was that you might straighten out what was left unfinished and appoint (ordain) elders in every town, as I directed you', and then follows a description of the characteristics of an elder.

Eldership has its roots in Judaism. It is the most ancient of all the church offices (Num. 11:16). In that early time God called out seventy men to share with Moses the task of caring for, providing for and protecting God's people, because the task was beyond the ability of one man to cope adequately and effectively. So plurality of leadership was born. Each synagogue had its elders who were responsible for worship, discipline and settling disputes. *Zaqen* (elder) of the Old Testament became *presbuteros* (elder) of the New Testament. Throughout Acts we have Jewish elders and Christian elders side by side – Acts 11:30; 14:23; 15:2,4,6,22,23; 20:17; 21:18 refer to the elders of the church; Acts 6:12; 4:23; 4:8; 4:5; 23:14; 24:1; 25:15 refer to the elders of the Jews. Quite obviously the elders in the Church were looked upon as having equal status in position and authority as elders were recognised to have in the synagogue, otherwise a word other than *presbuteros* would have been used.

In the New Testament elders are described as having the function of ruling. The word which is used to describe their function is *proistemi*. Literally it means 'to stand before'. It is used of the function of ruling within the local church fellowship in Romans 12:8 and in 1 Timothy 5:17 and within the context of a family in 1 Timothy 3:4 and 12. There are inevitable practical difficulties when it comes to selecting elders. Until we learn how to worship the Lord properly, wait upon him and allow the gifts of the Holy Spirit to operate realistically, these difficulties are not going to diminish, and we will need to resort to humans means of selection. However, the Bible does lay down some significant guidelines to enable our appreciation of the characteristics God is looking for in his elders – this we neglect at our peril. There are four areas which need to be reckoned with in recognising an elder. These areas emerge from 1 Timothy 3:1–7; Titus 1:5–9 and 1 Peter 5:2–4.

(a) *His Character* – God, as always, is much more concerned with what a man *is* than with what he *does*.

(b) *His Control* – with inescapable practical logic God indicates that it is absurd to expect a man to be responsible for and rule over the household of faith if his own domestic affairs are not in order.

(c) *His Competence* – in understanding, explaining and applying the word of God. This need not necessarily be in a public meeting, but certainly in a personal counselling situation.

(d) *His Commendation* – of Jesus Christ to the world, so that he will be the embodiment of the Gospel he declares and defends.

3. Poimēn

The shepherd or pastor will always be closely identified with the flock. In the West we often see sheep unattended as they roam the fields and hillsides, but in the East there is no flock without a shepherd. Sir George Adam Smith in his *Historical Geography of the Holy Land* says: 'With us sheep are often left to themselves; but I do not remember ever to have seen in the East a flock of sheep without a shepherd. In such a landscape as Judea, where a day's pasture is thinly scattered over an unfenced tract of country, covered with delusive paths, still frequented by wild beasts, and rolling off into the desert, a man and his own character are indispensable. On some high moor, across which at night the hyenas howl, when you meet him, sleepless, far-sighted, weather-beaten, armed, leaning on his staff, and looking out over his scattered sheep, every one of them on his heart, you understand why the shepherd of Judea sprang to the forefront of his people's history; why they gave his name to their king, and made him the symbol of providence; why Christ took him as the symbol of self-sacrifice.' His task within the flock is to be the spiritual paedeatrician – ensuring that the climate, diet, discipline, protection is right to enable the sheep to grow and develop so as to be pleasing and profitable to his master. His constant example is none other than the strong yet tender Shepherd of Israel. 'He tends his flock like a shepherd; he gathers the lambs in his arms and carries them close to his heart; he gently leads those that have young.' In order to do this properly, however, he needs to exercise his godly authority. In Bible times the shepherd was not only known for his ability to care for the flock, but also for his authority over them which was absolute. He does not lead where the majority of the sheep want to go, but where he knows, beyond any doubt, there is rich pasture, healthy, refreshing, and comparatively secure. In the well-known Psalm 23 you have this concept clearly expressed. 'Yahweh is my Shepherd'. In Ezekiel 34:1 and 2 'the word of the Lord came to me: Son of man, prophesy against the shepherds of Israel; prophesy and say to them: "This is what the Sovereign Lord says: Woe to the shepherds of Israel who only take care of themselves." Should not shepherds take care of the flock?' Clearly the kings and leaders of Israel are spoken of as shepherds. The verb from the noun *poimēn* is *poimainō* and it normally and correctly is translated 'to rule' (Matt. 2:6; Rev. 2:7; 12:5; 19:15). This verb indicates that the governing power exercised by the shepherd is to be of a firm character.

From all of this, leadership, quite clearly, is God-selected, congregationally accepted, and authoritatively implemented. The true leader is not responsible *to* the congregation, but he is responsible *for* the congregation *to* God. I heard of a Baptist minister who lovingly expressed his attitude to his congregation in this way: 'I will in every way, and at all times be your servant, but you can never, under any circumstances, be my master.' Such is the practical summary of the task of biblical leadership regardless of the tradition from which we come.

What kind of response needs to follow such a definition of leadership? The writer to the Hebrews does not mince his words when he says: 'Obey your leaders and submit to their authority' (Heb. 13:17). There are two reasons for this kind of response.

(a) *Divine.* We respond in this way of obedience and submission for the Lord's sake – not to give the leader some kind of power complex. The reaction of the leader's heart is his problem which he needs to work out before the Lord. The reaction of our hearts is a desire to do what the Lord wants. It is clearly stated in the midst of a very hostile social and political climate when Peter was writing to Christians who were undergoing severe persecution: 'Submit yourselves for the Lord's sake to every authority instituted among men: whether to the king, as the supreme authority, or to governors, who are sent by him to punish those who do wrong and to commend those who do right.' If that is to be our response in the political context to the ministers of God, how much more easily within the godly climate of the local church. We are so often obsessed with ourselves (admittedly we want to disguise this with our concern for others in the situation), and tacitly keep asking: 'What will this do for me/us?' 'Where does this leave me/us?' In fact we ought to be asking: 'What will this do for him (God)?' The reply to that question is that it will give him the desire of his heart, since that is what he requires of us. We have concentrated for such a long time on what God is *like* and what he can *do*, and we need now to pay much more attention to what God *wants*. Resistance, stubbornness, rebellion against godly leadership in the church is disregard of and disobedience to the revealed will of God.

How easy it is by attitude, if not by action, not only to live in disobedience yourself, but to encourage others to do so.

(b) *Human.* The other side of the divine implication is the human. We need to see that the leadership has a genuine love for the church. This is not a soft, sentimental thing, but by definition is a love which is concerned only for the highest, best and most for those loved. Its pattern and highest expression is the love of Jesus on the cross – so it is a love which is concerned not to *get*, but to *give*. It is a love which is quite impossible apart from the real ministry of the Holy Spirit filling the leader's heart. There are those who would attempt to injure, confuse, and discourage the church – and of those we need to be well aware – but the leadership of God is not of this kind. Again we need to see with wonder and humility the position the leadership has been put in by God – unenviable to be sure, but nevertheless real. The verb which the writer to the Hebrews uses to express the function of church leaders is the Greek word *hegeomai* (Heb. 13:7,13 and 24). This is the word which is used of secular rulers by Jesus in the gospels (Mark 13:9 and Luke 21:12).

Remember, too, that each leader will one day give an account before the Judgment Seat of Christ for the way he has fulfilled his office – this is a much more solemn and cautioning reality than any humanly constituted body which may well call him to account.

What will be the result of this kind of response by the Church to its leader's authority? It will be to gain maturity, stability, unity and knowledge (Eph. 4:11–16). In fact problems in the Church are basically leadership problems. Paul pleads with the church in Thessalonica: 'We beg you, our brothers, to pay proper respect to those who work among you, who guide and instruct you in the Christian life. Treat them with the greatest respect and love [because you like them? are attracted by them? agree with them? are temperamentally akin to them? No!] because of the work they do. Be at peace among yourselves.'

Jesus taught that to *have* authority it was necessary to recognise and *submit* to authority (Matt. 8:5–13). So not

125

only for the sake of our sanctification, but also for the sake of our relevant service this response to church leadership is necessary.

An obedient response to the leadership of the church has four main characteristics:

(a) *It is for the Lord's sake and not man's.* 'Submit yourselves for the Lord's sake to every authority instituted among men' (1 Pet. 2:13).

(b) *It is a response of love not fear.* 'Obey your leaders and submit to their authority. They keep watch over you as men who must give an account. Obey them so that their work will be a joy, not a burden, for that would be of no advantage to you' (Heb. 13:17).

(c) *It is voluntary not compulsive*, in that we are free to live God's way or not as we desire and then decide. 'It is for freedom that Christ has set us free. Stand firm, then, and do not let yourselves be burdened again by a yoke of slavery' (Gal. 5:1).

(d) *It is a response which is relative and not absolute* for only Christ can ultimately command absolute obedience.

Two further things need to be said. The first is that submission to authority is a sign of strength and not weakness. One of the great New Testament words is the word *praus* – often translated *meekness*. It really means strength which is now under control. It could be used of a wild horse which has been 'broken in' – and so is now responsive to the bit and bridle although it has lost nothing of its power or essential personality. In submission I demonstrate to myself, the devil, others, and God that I am looking beyond the human to the divine, and I am confident that God will honour his word and ultimately demonstrate his control over others in authority and honour all his promises. The second is that submission is a sign of Christ-likeness. He submitted to God, to the authorities both inside and outside the religion of his day, in earlier years to his parents at Nazareth – this was no facade, no token symbolic act.

> Lord bend that proud and stiff-necked I,
>   Help me to bow the head and die;

Beholding Him on Calvary
Who bowed His head for me.

It is so easy to speak of this in some vague, super-spiritual way – the reality, however, has to be worked out in a flesh and blood way. It is rather like the person who said: 'I do not mind being called a servant until somebody treats me like one.' The spirit of the world is stubbornness, and submission is the opposite of that. That is why the world denies it, the flesh recoils from it, and the devil hates it. To those called to Christian leadership as the Sleeping Giant stirs, Samuel Logan Brengle, himself a man of singular spiritual power, gives the direction to spiritual authority: 'It is not won by promotion, but by many tears and confessions of sin, and humblings and heart-searchings and self-surrender; a courageous sacrifice of every idol, a bold uncomplaining and uncompromising embracing of the cross. It is not gained by seeking great things for ourselves, but, like Paul, in counting those things which were gain, loss for Christ. That is a great price, but it must be paid by him who would be a real leader.'

9: Social concern

Arnold Toynbee, in his Gifford Lectures, pays generous tribute to the character of the early Christians. He writes: 'The Christian Church won the heart of the masses because it did more for the masses than was done for them by any one of the higher rival religions, or by either the imperial or the municipal authorities, and the Christians were the only people in the Roman Empire, except the professional soldiers, who were prepared to lay down their lives for the sake of an ideal.

The late Archbishop William Temple did a great deal in the United Kingdom to destroy the popular fantasy that the sacred and the secular, the spiritual and the natural, the visible and the invisible, the obvious and the intangible, are in sharp distinction. We have come to see that this distinction is neither biblical nor Christian; it is in fact Gnostic and Manichean in origin. It is based upon the false assumption that the spiritual is good while the material is evil and corrupt and does not take sufficiently into account the biblical teaching on the nature of man, the significance of creation or the scope of the Gospel. William Temple claimed that of all the great religions of the world Christianity was by far the most materialistically minded. More than Hinduism, Mohammedanism, even more than Judaism, it concerned itself with practical humanitarianism – with, for example, prison reforms, the Factory Acts, the emancipation of slaves and with the alleviation of human suffering wherever it was to be found. No Christian who takes the incarnation seriously can accept a rigid demarcation between the sacred and the secular. God made heaven and earth and the latter with all its fulness is his, and he sent Jesus Christ into the world, not only to redeem the individual soul, but to create a new community through which he would reveal himself and affect society as a whole.

Quite clearly the early Church which penetrated so deeply into society exhibited a willingness to alter its whole life-style under the dynamic Gospel. First of all it demonstrated a whole new attitude to life itself. Instead of seeing itself as living in the world and coming into the Church to 're-charge' its batteries, it saw itself as living in the Church and going out into the world as salt and light. There was a frequency of gathering for prayer, fellowship, and learning which assured this and which apparently is beyond our life-style in the West to grasp. Secondly, there was an expectancy that God by his Spirit would act. Most of the teaching in Acts is a consequence of a supernatural occurrence which raised questions which had to be answered satisfactorily. Thirdly, there was a deep concern for one another (*koinonia*) which expressed itself in sharing their possessions and their food together. What thrills me more than anything else is that this was not the result of a rule to be followed which would inevitably develop into arid legalism, but was the result of the transforming work of the Holy Spirit within them individually and corporately which resulted in a very practical mutual love and care. Barnabas seems to be Luke's visual aid for a positive example of this, while Ananias and Sapphira are an example of its abuse. The passages which summarise what went on in the early Church are Acts 2:43–7; 4:32–5:11. These are presumably not simply a description of local ideals, but descriptions of what Luke found to be going on wherever the Church expressed its life.

The Bible reveals God – when he took the initiative and liberated his people from their bondage in Egypt; through the warnings and pronouncements of the prophets; in the care and compassion of Jesus who responded to the material, tangible, physical needs of people so sensitively according to approximately two-thirds of the Gospel record; in the loving action of the early Church which was astonishingly radical – as a God of justice who is deeply concerned for the oppressed, underprivileged and the disadvantaged wherever they are found. Nothing could be clearer in this regard than the straightforward words of the beloved disciple of Christ towards the end of his earthly life: 'This is how we know what love is; Jesus Christ laid down his life for us and we ought to lay down our lives for others. If anyone has material possessions and sees his brother in need, but has no pity on him, how can the love of God be in him? Dear children, let us not love with words or tongue, but with actions and in truth' (1 John 3:16–18). It is easy – so easy – to rejoice in the Gospel of John 3:16 which give us the confident assurance that God loves us, but it is difficult – so difficult – to respond to the First Letter of John 3:16 and its challenge to practical and even painful compassion. The command to 'lay down our lives for our brothers' has so often been misused at a time of war. Most men and women go to war hoping that they will return – hoping that it will be the men and women of the enemy forces who will lay down their lives for their country. I am not critical of that attitude, but it is not the attitude we are called to by the Holy Spirit in 1 John 3:16. It means there that we are to be concerned and eager to give even when we could be absolutely free – and indeed when it may well be seen to be quite legitimate and socially acceptable – to keep. This is a happy, voluntary giving for the sake of enabling and enriching someone else who has a need which we can meet.

Ernest Gordon, who later became the Dean of Princeton University, in his remarkable book *Miracle on the River Kwai* tells a very moving story which occurred among the Allied prisoners of war who had been set to work in savage conditions by their Japanese captors on the Burma railway. He tells how morale was very low among the prisoners and how common decencies were set aside and the law of the jungle prevailed among them. It was a case of every man for himself. An incident occurred which transformed the whole atmosphere and outlook. Returning one day from their work on the railway, it was discovered that one of the tools they had been using was missing. The men were paraded, and the person responsible for the missing tool was asked to step forward. No one moved. The Japanese sergeant became increasingly irrational and threatened to shoot the whole company unless the guilty prisoner stepped forward. Suddenly, and deliberately, one man stepped out of the ranks. Immediately he was thrashed and clubbed to death by his captors. The squad was then marched back to camp. The tools were re-checked on return, and it was discovered that a mistake had been made, and in fact all the tools were accounted for. This revolutionised the camp.

This is partially the meaning of 1 John 3:16 – Jesus not only chose to be *born*, he also chose to *die*. Referring to Jesus the tense of the Greek verb is the Past Tense, which implies a once-for-allness about the act. It was a completed voluntary act in past time. Referring, however, to us in the light of the example of Jesus the tense of the Greek verb is the Present Tense, which implies a continual ongoing process. It is true that more people have died for their faith in this century than at any other period in history, but there is a routine, humdrum way of laying down (and going on laying down) your life for your brethren. That continual process is picked up in 1 John 3:17. 'If anyone has material possessions and sees his brother in need, but has no pity on him, how can the love of God be in him?' If we claim to be the people of God, one sure sign of the reality that we have in fact become partakers of God's nature is that we will have a practical and sacrificial concern for the poor. John, in his letter, goes further and questions the reality of real spiritual life within us where that concern is absent.

Ronald Sider in *Living More Simply* says:

The Old Testament does not tell us specifically whether we should buy a better car, keep the one we have or have no car at all. It does not tell us whether we should upgrade our life-style by getting a bigger house, or cut it back by getting a smaller one. It does not specify exactly what our life-style should be. Rather, it gives us certain principles by which we must measure our life-style. To face these principles honestly and prayerfully is bound to lead to changes that will help us simplify our lives in order to be more obedient disciples of our Lord.

Foundational to all that the Old Testament has to say is that God is a God of justice. Sometimes those who accept the Bible as the real revelation of the heart of God to man have been hesitant and even remote from this expression of his nature as it lays responsibility on them. Many, indeed, have concluded that the Bible has little to say about justice. This may well arise from the fact that still there is the strong foundation of the Authorised Version (King James) translation of the Bible in our understanding. The Hebrew word for *justice* which is used far more than any other in the Old Testament is *mishpat*. In the Authorised Version *mishpat* is translated *judgment* 294 times and only once is it translated *justice*. In over 90 of these 294 occasions, however, *mishpat* means *justice* and in fact in more recent translations of the Bible it is translated in this way. For example, in Psalm 106:3, 'Blessed are they who maintain justice' is 'Blessed are they who keep judgment'; Isaiah 30:18, 'The Lord is a God of justice' is 'The Lord is a God of judgment'; and Amos, who is outstanding and outspoken in proclaiming the word of the Lord against oppression and injustice, in Amos 5:24 'Let justice roll down like waters' is diluted to 'Let judgment roll down like waters'. Although two other Hebrew words (*tsedeq* and *tsedaqah*) are used in the Old Testament and the Authorised Version (King James) does translate them as *justice* on 25 occasions, the main cutting edge of the revelation of God as a God of justice is blunted. The emphasis on this cardinal characteristic of the nature of God is obscured. This emphasis is always linked to the need for a simple and considerate life-style. And so the impact of this practical consequence is significantly reduced.

The greatest thing that has ever been said about humanity is that the source of our human dignity does not lie in our position or our possessions, nor in our insights or achievements, but in the fact that, though defaced and deformed by the Fall and beyond human power to repair, God created us in his image. 'God said, "Let us make man in our image, in our likeness, and let them rule over the fish of the sea and the birds of the air, over the livestock, over all the earth, and over all the creatures that move along the ground." So God created man in his own image, in the image of God he created him; male and female, he created them' (Gen. 1:26–7). The implications of this are far-reaching. In the light of it we need with honesty to consider if there is anything we do, in the way we live, which contributes to the diminishing or the degrading of our fellow human beings, and if there is any way at all by which we might enhance and enrich the lives of those who are destitute and disadvantaged since they too are created in the image of God to display his glory, and God requires justice from us towards them.

C S Lewis in his sermon 'The Weight of Glory' says:

> The dullest and most uninteresting person you talk to may one day be a creature which, if you saw it now, you would be strongly tempted to worship, or else a horror and a corruption such as you now meet, if at all, only in a nightmare. . . You have never talked to a mere mortal. Nations, cultures, arts, civilisations, (and, may I interpose, all the trappings of affluence) – these are mortal, and their life is to ours as the life of a gnat. But it is immortals whom we joke with, work with, marry, snub, and exploit – immortal horrors or everlasting splendours.

God has created a world of abundance which he gave mankind to subdue and enjoy, but at the same time this world continues to be God's possession and we are here to share with eagerness and justice what he has provided for all of his creation. We need to reconsider our wasteful use of much of our God-given natural resources and adopt a lifestyle which would give credibility to our acknowledgement of this.

The Old Testament demands the law of tithing to be observed among God's people (Lev. 27:30–3; Num. 18:21–23; Deut. 12:5–18; Deut. 14:22–9). The implications of this are clear. Since the 'first-fruits' of anything is always regarded as special and so commands the highest price (even in today's markets) tithing implied that everything which humanity possesses first of all belongs to God. Inherent in this law is the concern to provide for the Lord's servants so that the 'government of God' would be maintained and for those disadvantaged and exposed through circumstances so that they could no longer provide or provide adequately for themselves. Closely related to the law of tithing was the law of gleaning (Lev. 19:9–10; Deut. 24:19–21). In practice it meant that the harvest of grain and fruit should not be totally gathered so that the poor and hungry would share in what God's earth had produced without any liability towards those who had prepared the soil, sown the seed, protected the crop, or finally harvested it.

Scripture neither idealises poverty nor does it condemn wealth and prosperity as evil in themselves, but it does command us to take responsibility for the needs of all men everywhere. The Church has awakened again to this area of responsibility as life has begun to stir within her. In 1974 in the Lausanne Congress for World Evangelisation – probably the largest, most representative international gathering of Christians ever assembled, issued and affirmed the Great Commission of Christ once more to 'go and make disciples of all nations'. The Congress explored the wide variety of means whereby a realistic and effective response could be made to this in the late twentieth century. One of these powerful means was an awareness by affluent Christians that they would begin to live a much simpler life-style. Paragraph 9 of the Lausanne Convenant reads:

All of us are shocked by the poverty of millions and disturbed by the injustices which cause it. Those of us who live in affluent circumstances accept our duty to develop a simple life-style in order to contribute generously to relief and evangelism.

Significantly, the Lausanne Covenant emphasises that the proper motivation for living more simply is not a commitment to a simple life-style, but a renewed commitment to

134

our Lord Jesus Christ and the establishment of his Kingdom on earth as it is in heaven and so our commitment to participate at every possible level in the mission of the King to redeem a lost and broken world. The over-riding factor in it all is that while the Church is growing more rapidly today than at any other time in her history, there are still two and a half billion people who have never heard the Gospel and up to one billion who are either starving or undernourished, and they are our responsibility and for them we will be accountable. Over 60 per cent of those two and a half billion people who have not yet heard of the grace of our Lord Jesus Christ live in social groupings and sub-nations where the Church has not yet effectively taken root. It is to these that Jesus says: 'Go.' We must respond, not because of their need both spiritually and materially, but simply because failure to respond would be blatant disobedience and insubordination. As the Sleeping Giant stirs one of the most pressing questions is 'will you dare realistically to measure the motivation and detail of your life-style by the needs of the poor and the unevangelised rather than by the living standards of your affluent neighbours?' Am I going to live more simply in order that others might simply live – not only on earth, but also in heaven?

Just over a mile from our church building is the headquarters of the Worldwide Evangelization Crusade. It is an old property which among many other distinguished figures in history was owned and occupied at one time by the notorious Judge Jeffries. It is set in about eighty acres of magnificent parkland which in the springtime and the autumn has a fragrance and a beauty which could never leave even the most insensitive and unappreciative unaffected. Immediately to the left inside the very imposing entrance is a very simple chapel. It has little symbolism to declare its use, but there many have fought spiritual battles and the grace of the Lord Jesus Christ has helped them and the peace of God has come. On the wall on the right hand side is a row of large framed photographs. These are the men and women of WEC who were in the Belgian Congo in 1964 when, following the assassination of Mr Patrice Lumumba,

135

who had formed the National Congolese Movement and won widespread support and devotion in the North East of the country, a new leader, Christophe Gbenye emerged and attacked Mwilu province. So began an armed internal conflict which had been simmering since the Belgian Government had given independence to the Congo in 1960. With the break-up of law and order and effective security age-old customs of witchcraft and cannibalism returned. The missionaries were caught in this seething cauldron of nationalism and the powers of darkness.

One of these was twenty-eight year old Bill McChesney. He had gone to Congo from Phoenix, Arizona, and had been there from 1960 just prior to Congo's Independence. His responsibilities included the maintenance and repair of vehicles which were used by the mission. During the occupation of the area where he was working by the Rebel forces he became a target of antagonism and hatred because of his nationality, and from time to time he was held in custody, severely beaten, and became a sick man. On 25 November, he was again arrested at the mission location. One missionary recalls the event: 'He looked like a young schoolboy being marched off by the five or more Simba guards.' There appears to be some uncertainty about how Bill died. None of the missionaries actually saw it happen. However *Time* magazine of 8 January, 1965, reported:

According to survivors, the Simbas raced around screeching, 'Kill, kill, kill them all!' The Belgians were shot, clubbed to death, or tied up and hurled into the Samba River. But that was killing with kindness compared to the fate of American Protestant missionary William McChesney, 28. They performed a mad war dance on his prostrate body until internal bleeding from ruptured organs ended his agony. Then the Simbas plucked out his eyes and threw his corpse into the river.

In what might be regarded as poor poetry Bill McChesney shares the choice which he made in life and calls it simply 'My Choice'. Whatever the literary verdict on the poem,

the spiritual impact is profound since this man was prepared
to put his life where his words were.

MY CHOICE

I want my breakfast served at 'Eight',
  With ham and eggs upon the plate;
A well-broiled steak I'll eat at 'One',
  And dine again when day is done.

I want an ultra-modern home,
  And in each room a telephone;
Soft carpets, too, upon the floors,
  And pretty drapes to grace the doors.

A cosy place of lovely things,
  Like easy chairs with inner springs,
And then I'll get a small TV –
  Of course, 'I'm careful what I see'.

I want my wardrobe, too, to be,
  Of neatest, finest quality,
With latest style in suit and vest.
  Why shouldn't Christians have the best?

But then the Master I can hear,
  In no uncertain voice, so clear.
'I bid you come and follow me,
  The lowly man of Galilee.

Birds of the air have made their nest,
  And foxes in their holes find rest;
But I can offer you no bed;
  No place have I to lay my head.'

In shame I hung my head and cried.
  How could I spurn the crucified?
Could I forget the way He went,
  The sleepless nights in prayer He spent?

For forty days without a bite,
  Alone He fasted day and night;
Despised, rejected – on He went,
  And did not stop till veil He rent.

A man of sorrows and of grief,
  No earthly friend to bring relief –
'Smitten by God', the prophet said –
  Mocked, beaten, bruised, His blood ran red.

If He be God and died for me,
  No sacrifice too great can be
For me, a mortal man, to make;
  I'll do it all for Jesus' sake.

Yes, I will tread the path He trod,
  No other way will please my God;
So, henceforth, this my choice shall be,
  My choice for all eternity.

However much we try to cushion and dilute the challenge of Jesus, the fact remains that his teaching uncompromisingly demands a radical commitment to the Kingdom of God. Often misunderstood, nevertheless his call to us disdains half-hearted lukewarmness, and comes into conflict with the tenderest and most personal duties (Matt. 13:44–6; Luke 9:57–62). He plainly assures us that if we look after his things then he will look after ours as far as diet and dress, and presumably the kind of house we live in, car we drive and holidays we need are concerned (Matt. 6:24–34; 7:7–12). The teaching of Jesus on wealth and possessions is not that they are in themselves wrong, but they have an inherent tendency to root us in the wrong place. There is an alleged saying of Jesus which is not in the Bible, yet is in keeping with his teaching, which is: 'The world is a bridge – the wise man crosses over it while the foolish man builds upon it.' Those who consistently keep their money, no matter how honestly it is earned, are condemned by Jesus (Luke 12:13–21; 16:19–31). Any radical and so real commitment to Jesus as Lord will result in a life-style of giving, since giving and hoarding are mutually exclusive options. Jesus loved and therefore gave; we are also to love and therefore to give. The hand that remains closed in the presence of need must inevitably reveal a heart which is still ignorant of the real Jesus, a life in which Jesus is anything but Lord.

It is so easy for us in the West unconsciously to accept a largely middle-class culture and life-style as the norm, with its worldly values and selfish ambitions, and conveniently ignore the radical teaching of Jesus concerning money, possessions and social standing and so to become in attitude if not in activity quite indistinguishable from the covetous world around us. We, as Christians, even try with high-sounding, spiritual reasons, to justify the money we spend on our homes, food, clothes, possessions, antiques, entertainments, holidays, education, and even church buildings. We speak of 'trying to win our friends for Christ' and 'nothing less than the best is good enough for God' and 'the church buildings must reflect the beauty and glory of our Creator' while often in fact these same buildings and outward palaver are 'to the glory of man and in loving memory of God'. Frequently it all adds up to an attempt to offset our conscious concern over the poverty of our spiritual lives and our patent failure to manifest the life of Jesus in the power of the Holy Spirit through these mortal bodies of ours which are the dwelling places of that same Holy Spirit.

As the Sleeping Giant has begun to stir there are three areas where challenges have come. Because of our unfamiliarity with these areas glaring mistakes have been made and fears have arisen. It is so easy to become critical of those who have begun to move out and on in faith into these areas where there is so little modern precedent to guide and correct. How we need a fresh baptism of love to motivate ourselves and encourage others in the power of the Holy Spirit to walk with him who, though he was rich, for our sakes became poor in order that we might become rich. We may indeed become poor for a variety of reasons, but seldom deliberately and with godly forethought in order that others who are poor might become rich.

The *first* area of challenge is inevitably at a deeply personal level. We need to come to realistic terms with the fact that most of us could live far more simply than we do – not in a martyr or pharisaical spirit, but in a spirit of joyful submission to the revealed will of God. If what we claim for the Gospel is going to have any credibility then we need to admit that our lives are often controlled and dominated much more by Western culture and social convention than by biblical standards. Paul, writing out of a very full heart, to the Christians at Corinth says: 'At the present time your plenty will supply what they need, so that in turn their plenty will supply what you need. Then there will be equality. . .' (2 Cor. 8:14). In the early Church the principle which operated among God's people was equality. However hard that may be to define, the principle remains before us to be embraced – I think only possible in the supernatural power of the Holy Spirit. In the very next chapter Paul enunciates the second biblical principle which is to govern our life-style personally: 'And God is able to make all grace abound to you, so that in all things at all times, having all that you need, you will abound in every good work.' Everything which is more than 'all that you need' is to enable us to 'abound in every good work'. So 'equality' and 'all that you need' is the biblical standard set for each Christian. Sometimes the difficulty of determining how to work the biblical standard out in practical terms is so great that we do not even begin to try. Of course it is much more acceptable to hide in the difficulty rather than face up to the demand which it poses.

John Wesley faced the biblical standard in his own life and gave his own response in one of his frequently repeated sermons on Matthew 6:19–23. He claimed that Christians should give away all but the 'plain necessaries of life' – plain, wholesome food, clean clothes and enough to carry on his business. He strongly counselled that a man should earn what he could by honest and just means. Having satisfied the bare necessities of life the poor should receive the remainder. Wesley's observation was that there was not 1 person in 500 in any 'Christian city' who obeys Jesus' command. He saw this as a clear demonstration that most professing believers were 'living men, but dead Christians'. Wesley insisted that any 'Christian' who takes for himself anything more than the 'plain necessaries of life' is in fact living 'in an open, habitual denial of the Lord' and has 'gained riches and hell-fire'. However difficult it may be for many to receive this teaching, two things impress me. One is that Wesley himself lived out his own teaching. Sales of his books often earned him £1,400 annually, but he spent less than £30 on himself. He gave the rest away. He wore inexpensive clothes and ate simple food. He once wrote, 'If I leave behind me £10, you and all mankind bear witness against me that I lived and died a thief and a robber.' The other thing that impressed me is that God used Wesley in an extraordinarily effective way to revive a decadent Church and rescue a whole nation from devastating riots and shedding of blood. I cannot but believe that there is a connection between one and the other.

One of the four main influences on my life as a preacher, Dr James S Stewart, formerly Professor of New Testament at New College in Edinburgh, says in his book *Thine is the Kingdom*: 'St Paul in his day had to appeal to the Roman Christians not to be conformed to the world, but rather to be transformed by the renewing of their minds, for only to a Church radically different from the world will the world consent to listen; and the whole cause of the Kingdom of God, now as then, is at stake in that appeal.' By a radical re-appraisal of our life-style personally we need to validate, symbolise and facilitate our concern for those who are hungry in body, mind and spirit.

The *second* area of challenge is not so much on an individual basis as on a corporate level so that together as a fellowship we can present a new pattern to society which will visibly demonstrate to a divided world how it is possible to live together in meaningful and loving relationships. The one thing that the world has failed to do throughout its history is to live together in a significant way. All the way there is division domestically, socially, economically, politically, racially, and even ecclesiastically. Rather pretentiously we claim, as Christians, that we have discovered the way to live in harmony with one another. When man quarrelled with God in Genesis 3, it was inevitable that in

Genesis 4, as night follows day, man would quarrel with man. When Jesus died on the cross he not only potentially put man into a new and right relationship with God, but also into a new and right relationship with his brother man. Our task and responsibility is to live out the reality of that divine accomplishment in our lives. Many have the theology right but find a serious shortfall in practice. Ronald Sider appraises the situation in the Church today in this way:

> Things are more important than persons. Job security and an annual salary increase matter more than starving children and oppressed peasants. . . Biblical revelation summons us to defy many of the basic values of our materialistic, adulterous society.

> But that is impossible! As individuals, that is. It is hardly possible for isolated believers to resist the anti-Christian values which pour forth from our radios, TVs and advertising hoardings. The values of our affluent society seep slowly and subtly into our hearts and minds. The only way to defy them is to immerse ourselves deeply in Christian fellowship so that God can fundamentally re-mould our thinking, as we find our primary identity with our brothers and sisters who are also unconditionally committed to biblical values. . . For the early Christians *koinonia* was not the frilly 'fellowship' of church-sponsored, bi-weekly outings. It was not tea, biscuits and sophisticated small-talk in the Fellowship Hall after the sermon. It was an unconditional sharing of their lives with the other members of Christ's body.

> Christian fellowship means unconditional availability to and unlimited liability for the other sisters and brothers – emotionally, financially and spiritually.

It is to this deliberate and inevitably painful reality that I am called to live in the power of the Holy Spirit. I enter into it knowing that it will affect not only me, but also my family and my future. But what will be the effect? The Body of Christ will be seen to function as the reality which

God intended, and being a truly prophetic word to the society which it serves.

The *third* area of challenge goes beyond any personal and corporate attempts to live out a simpler life-style according to biblical standards. We have formed structures within our society which have encouraged the evils of injustice, selfishness and neglect – and we have been party to these passively if not actively. Any serious repentance will involve us not only in kneeling in front of the church with tears, but in taking whatever means are available to change the structures which have encouraged these evils.

There are many within the Body of Christ who are aware of the evil within our society and desperately want to do something about it, but have such a deep-seated suspicion and scepticism that nothing can be done, especially by the Church, that in time they tend to degenerate into limp sentimentalism which imagines that a mere intellectual interest in social affairs can substitute for moral inertia and social inaction. Herbert Agar, in that clarion-sounding book *A Time for Greatness*, argues that the supreme need of the hour is not for one or two outstanding figures of vision and initiative, but for great living and high thinking on the part of common people.

A Communist once threw out this challenge to a Christian:

The Gospel is a much more powerful weapon for the renewal of society than is our Marxist philosophy, but all the same it is we who will finally beat *you*. . . We communists do not play with words. We are realists, and seeing that we are determined to achieve our object, we know how to obtain the means. Of our salaries and wages we keep only what is strictly necessary, and we give up our free time and part of our holidays. You, however, give only a little time and hardly any money for the spreading of the Gospel of Christ. How can anybody believe in the supreme value of this Gospel if you do not practise it, if you do not spread it, and if you sacrifice neither time nor money for it. . .? We believe in our

Communist message and we are ready to sacrifice everything, even our life. . . But you people are afraid even to soil your hands.

All over the world there is a real concern about personal Christian life-style, particularly in the affluent West, realistic relationships within the Body of Christ, and a loving defiance and insistent demand for change where social structures protect and promote social injustice.

10: Healing

Some years ago I was first confronted with the possibility that the Church in the twentieth century might be a powerful agent of God in accomplishing physical and emotional healing. My background made it second nature to pray in a prayer meeting with other Christians for the sick – but it tended to be formal, dutiful, and void of much confidence that healing would actually take place. The emphasis was rather on the fact that God would give grace to bear the sickness rather than secure healing. The exclusive hope for health which seemed to be realistically believed lay in the medical profession – and rightly prayer was offered that the doctors might do their job properly. I am convinced that God can and does use orthodox medicine to bring relief from suffering and often a return to health and normal living – and I want to pay my own tribute to the skill and devotion of those who are involved in the practice of medicine. However, my wife – a qualified doctor who graduated in Medicine from Edinburgh University with some distinction – had been reading the Acts of the Apostles and some monthly magazines which came by post to our home unasked for and with alarming regularity. Our children were young, and I was frequently out in the evening while she was at home. On my return in the evenings she started asking searching questions when I would much rather have watched television and gone to bed. The effect on me was disturbing, since here she was, the doctor, cross-examining me, the minister, about miraculous healing by God. Her questions were Bible-based and I sensed would lead me logically to a whole new dimension of ministry if they were followed through with integrity. The turmoil was not simply theological and intellectual, but had a strong emotional ingredient since a few years previously my mother had died from a particularly ugly form of cancer. Had I not prayed for her? Had not the church to which we belonged prayed for her? Had she not been a particularly fine Christian woman who loved and served God? And nothing had happened. She had died in physical humiliation and left me, an undergraduate, to cope with considerable disillusionment. The day came – unnoticed by me – when the questions stopped. My wife, Anne, had concluded that if God wanted to teach me about healing then *he* would have to do it since she seemed to making little progress.

Some months later God did – on the golf-course on the delightful Island of Cumbrae just off the West coast of Scotland. There was nothing particularly dramatic about it, only the dawning of a deep inner certainty that God was in many of the things we had talked about and I had read for myself. Since that summer afternoon I have never seriously doubted that the Lord wants to use his body on earth, the Church, to minister healing in such a way that he will be glorified. That is not to say that doubts have never come. Perhaps no area of ministry has so humbled me as this one. I am constantly aware that I am in contact here, not with theological concepts only, but with very tender and vulnerable personal relationships.

As a church here our first real entry into this ministry left many unanswered questions. Derek was a strong, gracious, self-effacing executive with an oil company. He was a family man in his mid-forties. By the time I got to know him he already had had surgery and therapy for cancer of the throat. By these methods the disease seemed to be kept in check, until yet another growth appeared in his neck. The prognosis was bad and the proposed treatment was a laryngectomy (the removal of his voice-box). Typical of Derek's courage and dignity, he felt that enough surgery had been done, and any further interference in his body would be for him a de-humanising process. It was a deeply personal conclusion to arrive at, and the consequences were faced. Things eventually took their course, and an inability to eat solids was followed by severe difficulty in swallowing liquids, and ultimately breathing itself became an alarming struggle. I visited him in hospital in London and in a mood more of desperation than faith called for the church elders to come and minister to him in the terms of James 5:14–16. We had never as an eldership exercised this ministry together before. I would like to be able to say that the very obvious swelling on Derek's neck subsided before our eyes – it didn't! But in a comparatively short time he was discharged from hospital and able to eat meat once more. Towards the end of that year, although physically still weak, he 'gave away' his daughter in marriage and hosted the wedding reception in their home. Within two days, however, Derek was dead – the result of a massive haemorrhage in his chest.

I lived for many months in confused silence. Not only had I parted from a man whom I had come to respect and admire, but also from someone who had become a very dear friend. I carried many painful questions in my heart that would not be silenced and even some basic tenets of the Faith came under the closest scrutiny in my mind. The years that have passed since then have not resolved all of these issues – and as a church we have known 'failure' as well as 'success' in the ministry of healing. I have had to return again and again to the Scriptures themselves for encouragement and strength in this whole area and, at the same time, I have drawn immense encouragement from the writings of others. Francis MacNutt, in his book on healing writes:

Since then I have seen many people healed – especially when I have prayed with a team or in a loving community. Although I travel too much to be able to follow up and estimate accurately, I would make a rough estimate that about half those we pray for are healed (or are notably improved) and about three-fourths of those we pray for are healed of emotional or spiritual problems. I say this as an encouragement for others to consider the possiblity that God might use their prayers someday to heal the sick.

That half are not healed as a result of ministry is a solace, although not an answer, to my questioning; that half are healed as a result of ministry is a challenge to my faith. I find that many Christians dwell on either the 'failure' half or the 'success' half in an exclusive way – and so arrive at an unbalanced and dishonest conclusion. Both need to be held before us with integrity in order that one might be a challenge and encouragement to the other to improve our spiritual performance.

I have struggled with the fact that many good and godly Christians have faith for sickness but not for healing – when all is said and done. There seems to be a desire to select passages of Scripture to feed *doubt* rather than *faith* (and you can use Scripture to feed either). How often have I heard Paul's *thorn* being cited as an example of how we are to deal with sickness (2 Cor. 12:1–10). This, in Paul's autobiography, is unlikely anyway to be a reference to physical sickness. Those who are convinced that it is refer to the phrase 'in my flesh' as evidence of some physical ailment. If we are to take this as literally true then we need to be logical and take 'a thorn' as literally true too. It is not, of course, literally 'a thorn in my flesh' but is a metaphor used by a man saturated in the Scriptures of the Old Testament. The idiom of 'a thorn in the flesh' is used there to refer to those who create difficulty and opposition (Num. 33:55; Jdg; 2:3; Josh. 23:13) for the people of God. The word 'messenger' is the Greek word *angelos* which always carries with it the idea of personal being rather than the abstract concept of physical disease. Quite clearly the context in which this personal testimony is given by Paul is that of opposition and obstruction by those who reject the message and so resist the messenger (2 Cor. 12:10). Other favourite passages which are used to feed doubt and uncertainty regarding healing are the references to Timothy's stomach (1 Tim. 5:23), the illness of Trophimus which meant he had to remain at Miletus (2 Tim. 4:20), and the almost fatal illness of Epaphroditus (Phil. 2:27). Perhaps the best known and most quoted of all is the uncomfortable and sad situation of Job in the Old Testament. But in his case, although the book of Job is comparatively long, the time which it covers is not, and in any case it was written to show the healing and deliverance which God wrought, so vindicating himself.

It seems to me that often so-called Christian maturity is characterised by pessimism, and hope – that foundation-stone of our Faith – is condemned to spiritual obscurity. Oscar Wilde makes a very shrewd observation in his time:

> In the English Church a man succeeds not through his capacity for belief, but through his capacity for disbelief. Ours is the only Church where the sceptic stands at the altar, and where St Thomas is regarded as the ideal apostle.

As the Sleeping Giant stirs there is a new awareness that faith is being called for by God – not in man with all his experience, skill, and even godliness, but in the word of God. Jesus spoke of faith as being like a grain of mustard seed (and that is often our refuge and retreat when our faith is weak and almost non-existent). But even a tiny mustard seed grows. It can become a tree eight to twelve feet high. One Sunday morning, during our morning Bible School, we passed a basket full of mustard seeds round our crowded congregation. Some lost them before the day was out; some fixed them to the cover of their Bibles; but some planted them. After some weeks one family eventually brought quite a significant mustard plant to church. We discovered that in order to grow the mustard seed needs the right soil, the right climate, and the right feeding. So it is with faith – it requires the soil of fellowship (a fellowship which will minister encouragement and not discouragement, hope and not despair); it requires the climate of God-awareness for we are not living in the Kingdom of darkness nor the Kingdom of man; and it requires to be fed by the word of God.

Two visitors spent a Sunday in a parish about thirty-five

minutes car ride from us and at the end of that day said to the vicar: 'Our people believe the Word of God – your people believe the Word of God works.' The key lies in our willingness to receive the word of God with faith and then work it out in the power of the Holy Spirit. The heroes of faith, not only in the Bible, but also throughout history staked everything on God – and history has proved them right. Faith's chief occupation is the obtaining of the promises of God. Faith is always discovering what God is able to do in the face of opposition and difficulty. Faith is willing to accept what it cannot understand. To doubt any word which God has spoken is to cripple faith, for faith is neither discouraged nor encouraged by circumstances. It is with a considerable awe in my soul that I have come to see that unbelief is represented in Scripture as the one and only thing which exasperates God.

As far as healing is concerned, the weight of Scripture is quite overwhelming. God is unequivocally presented as a God who is able to heal (and our categorising of disease may facilitate our thinking, but often ministers doubt and plain unbelief). 'Praise the Lord, O my soul, and forget not all his benefits. He forgives all my (your) sins and heals all my (your) diseases' cries the psalmist in an outburst of praise and joy (Ps. 103:2,3). 'My son, pay attention to what I say; listen closely to my words. Do not let them out of your sight, keep them within your heart; for they are life to those who find them and health to a man's whole body.' That is the quite staggering claim made by the writer of Proverbs (Prov. 4:20–2). The heart-broken, weeping prophet Jeremiah declares an incredible thing when he says: 'Ah, Sovereign Lord.. . . Nothing is too hard for you.' The angel Gabriel, sent directly to earth from God with the news of the incarnation, underlines that very same reality to an apprehensive, uncomprehending Mary with great authority: 'For nothing is impossible with God' (Lk. 1:37) – not even a terminal illness; an ugly deformity; or an incurable·disease. As far as Abraham was concerned (and he was the embodiment of faith) there were two ingredients in his faith. He believed first of all that God can create something out of nothing and secondly that God can bring to life what is dead.

Not only, however, does the Bible present God as a God who is able to heal, but also as a God who *wants* to heal. The only time God *sent* sickness was when the people of God rebelled and resisted their leaders. This, too, is a very solemn and awesome reality. God's ideal, and so his desire, is that everything should function properly. When he created the world – including man – there was no shadow of disease or sickness. 'God saw all that he had made and it was very good' (Gen. 1:31). This is the way God so clearly wanted it to be. Some time later, as he entered into a loving relationship with man, he secured that relationship with a covenant having freed his people from slavery. The words of his covenant are quite thrilling: 'He said, "If you listen carefully to the voice of the Lord your God and do what is right in his eyes, if you pay attention to his commands and keep all his decrees, I will not bring on you any of the diseases I brought on the Egyptians, for I am the Lord who heals you" ' (Exod. 15:26). 'Worship the Lord your God, and his blessings will be on your food and water. I will take away sickness from among you, and none will miscarry or be barren in your land. I will give you a full life span' (Exod. 23:25,26). If God affirms that he wants to heal under the terms of the Old Covenant he made with the Jewish people, surely he would desire at least that and so fulfil it under the New Covenant which has been made possible and confirmed through the blood of Christ. Speaking of the Old Testament saints and system, the writer to the Hebrew Christians says: 'But the ministry Jesus has received is as superior to theirs as the covenant of which he is mediator is superior to the old one, and it is founded on better promises' (Heb. 8:6). After all, the Old Covenant was based on Law, whilst the New Covenant is based on love; the Old Covenant was based on race, while the New Covenant is based on grace; the Old Covenant was based on what man can do, whilst the New Covenant is based on what God has done. So as he is creator and a covenant-keeping God we can affirm his desire to heal.

Of course, the summit of it all is reached in Jesus Christ. He came not only to redeem mankind, but also to reveal what God is like. On that tense emotional last night in Jerusalem before Jesus went down from the Temple area across the Kedron Valley and on to the Mount of Olives and Gethsemane there was an urgency about Jesus' teaching and the disciples' questioning. It was in this climate that Jesus responded to a questioning cry from Philip's heart by saying: 'Believe me when I say that I am in the Father, and the Father is in me; or at least believe on the evidence of the miracles themselves' (John 14:11).

Few people would think of Jesus apart from his healing ministry. Jesus quite clearly came to *do* and *reveal* God's will (John 4:34; 5:19,20,30; 6:38; 10:37,38; 14:10–12; Heb. 10:7,9). The record of the Gospels indicates that he healed all who came to him – there are twenty-six cases of individual healing and ten cases of multiple healings in the Gospel record. It is true that he did not heal everyone, but he appears to have healed everyone who came to him. Indeed, the only time that Jesus' willingness to heal is questioned by someone who came to him is in the first chapter of Mark. Jesus quickly gives confidence and re-assurance about what he wants: 'A man with leprosy came to him and begged him on his knees, "If you are willing, you can make me clean." Filled with compassion, Jesus reached out and touched the man. "I am willing" he said, "Be clean!" Immediately the leprosy left him and he was cured' (Mark 1:40–2).

Jesus went on to extend his own ministry and to ensure the future by calling around him a fellowship of people to whom he could give himself and then commission to go in his name. 'When Jesus had called the twelve together, he gave them power and authority to drive out all demons and to cure diseases, and he sent them out to preach the Kingdom of God and to heal the sick' (Luke 9:1,2). 'After this the Lord appointed seventy-two others and sent them two by two ahead of him to every town and place where he was about to go. . . Heal the sick who are there and tell them, "The Kingdom of God is near you" ' (Luke 10:1,9). Perhaps the most familiar passage of all that records Jesus' words is Matthew 28:18-20 which rings out its trumpet-toned commission in what the Duke of Wellington has called 'the marching orders of the Christian Church'. 'Then Jesus came to them and said, "All authority in heaven and on earth has been given to me. Therefore go and make disciples of all nations, baptising them in the name of the Father and of the Son and of the Holy Spirit, and teaching them to obey everything I have commanded you." ' What is the 'everything I have commanded you'? He commanded the disciples to do three things; to challenge the powers of darkness; to cure sickness and disease; and to communicate the Gospel of the Kingdom (cf. Mark 16:17,18; John 14:12; 20:21).

When the Gospel record is completed, the New Testament is strewn with evidence that the Lord's intention is that the ministry of healing should continue (e.g. 1 Cor. 12:7,9,28; Jas. 5:14-16). There is not only evidence of Jesus' intention, but there are many examples of his fulfilling this ministry through his servants (e.g. Acts 2:43; 5:12,15,16; 6:8; 8:4-8; 9:17,18; 14:3; 19:11,12; 28:8,9; Gal. 3:5; Heb. 2:4).

The Bible bears eloquent testimony to the fact that God is recognised as being present and active, praised and acknowledged, not in sickness but in healing (e.g. Matt. 9:8; 15:30,31; 21:14,15; Luke 7:14-16; 17:15; 18:43; Acts 3:8,9).

In addition to all of this, to examine a passage like Isaiah 53:4,5 in the light of Matthew 8:16,17 and 1 Peter 2:24 leaves no reasonable or honest doubt that Jesus dealt with sickness as well as sin when he poured out his life on the cross. Sickness is regarded in the Bible as being part of the curse of the Law (cf. Deut. 28:15, 21-8, 58-61) and Jesus is triumphantly declared to have suffered and died to rescue and redeem us from the curse of the Law (Gal. 3:13). Again, the Bible proclaims that sickness is a bondage of Satan (cf. Job 2:7; Luke 13:11-16; Acts 10:38) and that Jesus died in order to set us free, disentangle us, spring the trap (Isa. 61:1,2; Luke 4:18,19; John 8:31-36; 1 John 3:8;

Gal. 5:1; Col. 1:13,14; 2:15). In other words, healing is an integral part of the Gospel and the coming of the Kingdom of God (cf. Isa. 35:4-6; Matt. 10:8; 11:4,5; Mark 6:12,13; Luke 9:2; 10:9). Indeed, the Greek word *sozo* (and its compound form *diasozo*) is used for the healing of physical disease (16 times) as well as for salvation or healing of the whole person (94 times).

However demanding this reality is, and however difficult it is for us to grasp in the light of our personal experience, we are confronted inescapably with the evidence of Scripture and called upon to make a very significant choice – shall I trust my experience or shall I trust the word of God? It is this choice that has caused so much heartache and such a strong reaction. The gospels of Mark and Luke record the concept of the Kingdom of God on 116 occasions. It is not a geographical or political Kingdom which is being spoken of, but the area where the personal authority of God is being exercised. The Kingdom of God is seen wherever God's power and control reaches out, and wherever life in any of its aspects has been or is being touched by the power of God. You do not have to move house or change jobs or get on a boat or plane to live in the Kingdom of God. You are there the moment you allow God's power to get hold of and take control of your life according to his word and through the life and ministry of his Holy Spirit. One of the clear manifestations of the reality of the Kingdom of God being established among men is the healing of those who are sick: ' "As you go" Jesus said, "preach this message: the Kingdom of heaven is near. Heal the sick, raise the dead, cleanse those who have leprosy [that is, those who are beyond any help through human means], drive out demons. Freely you have received, freely give. . ." '

Biblically there are five main channels through which God will minister healing. Perhaps the two most familiar are the ministry of the elders of the Church and through prayer. In the letter of James, which was written almost certainly by the brother of our Lord to second generation Christians, we have a challenge to practical, visible Christianity. The letter to James is referred to as 'a description of true religion'. Dr G Campbell Morgan comments: 'That Word is only of real value as it is obeyed, as what it enjoins is done. There is no profit, but rather the reverse, in hearing, if there be no doing.' Writing about healing James says: 'Is any one of you sick? He should call the elders of the church to pray over him with oil in the name of the Lord. And the prayer offered in faith will make the sick person well; the Lord will raise him up. If he has sinned, he will be forgiven. Therefore confess your sins to each other and pray for each other that you may be healed. The prayer of a righteous man is powerful and effective.' So closely allied to the particular ministry of the elders is the more general ministry of prayer. How difficult it is really to accept the words of Jesus in a specific matter like physical healing when he says in a categorical way: 'Have faith in God. I tell you the truth, if anyone says to this mountain, "Go throw yourself into the sea", and does not doubt in his heart but believes that what he says will happen, it will be done for him. Therefore I tell you, whatever you ask for in prayer, believe that you have received it, and it will be yours. And when you stand praying, if you hold anything against anyone, forgive him, so that your Father in heaven may forgive you your sins' (Mark 11:22-6). This assurance by Jesus is given within the context of the strange occurance of the withered fig tree. Quite clearly by a word God can create or destroy; he can bless or blight. That is an awesome thing. It seems as if the disciples had as big a problem over the miraculous as we have many hundreds of years later – although they were there and had actually seen Jesus in action many times. They were witnesses to something which is quite outside man's power to achieve. Even the most experienced and able scientist cannot tell matter to do something and have it obey him. As ever it is Peter who is the spokesman: 'Look, Lord, the fig tree you spoke to yesterday?' To this Jesus replies in these momentous words of Mark 11:22-6.

There appear to be two conditions for such remarkable power in prayer. The first condition is *faith*. Faith is defined here as the absence of doubt in the heart. There are two things of which we need to be absolutely certain before we can have this quality of faith in our praying. These are *could God do it?* and *will God do it?* These are two separate questions. If we could pray in faith that is certain and entertains no doubt that God *could* do it, and that God *will* do it, then we have the promise of Jesus that it will happen. It is as simple and as difficult as that. In the technology/ science orientated twentieth century it is difficult for us to believe often that God *could* do it. It is often even more difficult for us to be sure that God really *wants* to do it. Prayer is not some kind of test – but rather giving God an entrance into a situation to do entirely as he desires. However, if we are absolutely certain about these two things – the *power* of God to do it, and the *purpose* of God in doing it – we have the word of Christ that it will happen. The other condition is *forgiveness*. Jesus underlines this in a number of different contexts when he is speaking about effective praying. He emphasises so clearly that in prayer our concern is not just about the miraculous, but also about the moral – it is not just *faith* that needs to be present, but *forgiveness* too. If I am out of fellowship with my brother then I am also out of fellowship with my Father, and the channel is blocked – and prayer is unheard.

The other three channels by which God wants to minister his healing life are through spiritual gifts (1 Cor. 12:9); by the laying on of hands (Mark 16:18); and through biblical fellowship (Matthew 18:19,20). With regard to the first of these we have a doctor within our Fellowship who has a quite remarkable testimony to the reality of spiritual gifts being used in healing. Dr Edwards was born in Sri Lanka and lived in the capital city of Colombo. She is the eldest of a closely-knit family of five children, and was raised in a climate of nominal Christianity. She read Medicine in Colombo from 1961–1967 and then proceeded to do her pre-registration year before qualifying in 1969. During this time she says 'my understanding of Christianity was to do good works, but I did not believe much in prayer or regular church attendance.' She was transferred to a hospital 120 miles away from the family home, and it was there in

February of the following year she heard of the illness of her twenty-three-year-old second sister, Carmini. Carmini had been reading Accountancy in Colombo when she suddenly became ill with what seemed to be 'flu'. However, her condition deteriorated and typhoid, T.B., malaria, and rheumatic fever were all regarded and explored as possible sources of her illness. She was hospitalised and tests for all of these were carried out – but all were negative. Two months passed and her symptoms gave reason for real concern. Her temperature rose considerably and severe pain and swelling had now come to her joints. Fresh symptoms had begun to appear – bleeding from the gums and skin, and blood and proteins in the urine. She rapidly became anaemic and very weak, and blood transfusions gave only a short temporary improvement. Dr Edwards confesses that this was a very difficult time for her – she was 250 miles away from her sister and communication was difficult. Carmini was referred to a number of specialists and intense investigations continued. Blood tests, liver biopsy, and bone marrow biopsy eventually divulged the true nature of her condition. Dr Edwards was called into the physician's office in early July 1970, and was told that her sister was suffering from systemic lupus Erithematosis which is one of the collagen diseases. Her reaction was one of shock and panic, since she had seen a doctor suffer and die from this condition during her undergraduate days – it is a crippling, incapacitating disease which creeps progressively towards death. As a doctor she knew, too, of no medical treatment which could cure it, and apart from steroids little medication could helpfully be administered.

She went to her church and asked for help, but returned angry and disillusioned when she was told that miracles happened 2,000 years ago, but not today. Her anger was directed towards God since she felt that the Bible had given her false hopes. In this frame of mind she and her family turned to occult and other practices – but her sister's condition continued to deteriorate. Carmini was transferred to Colombo and arrived there on the 7 August, 1970. Her body had become distended as a result of steroid therapy, and her joints continued to be swollen and very painful; her gums continued to bleed; her hair had begun to fall out; and her temperature was around 106°F on average. She begged to be allowed home to die, and at the end of August she lost consciousness. The physician who cared for her gave her twenty-four hours to live, since there was no way of giving her drugs or intravenous therapy.

So decisive was the situation that friends and relatives had begun to arrive from different parts of the country for the funeral. That evening, however, another pastor called at their home at the request of one of Carmini's other sisters. He shared with the family what the Bible had to say about healing and asked them to believe with him for a miracle. He went to Carmini's beside and prayed for her. Dr Edwards shares her reaction to this: 'I stood there inwardly mocking all that he shared with us.' The pastor asked the family to continue with the medical treatment that was being given until the doctors on their own told Carmini that she was well.

Dr Edwards takes up the story again: 'Next morning to my amazement I found my sister conscious. Her temperature had come down and she looked cheerful and well. However, my medical knowledge gave a good explanation of that too – it was obviously an unusual remission. Gradually, however, she started recovering and towards the end of the year she was perfectly normal – although still on a small dose of steroid.' She tells of beginning to attend the church where the pastor who had ministered to Carmini was in leadership. She was intrigued to see the gifts of the Holy Spirit operating in a New Testament pattern. She tells of the continuing struggle, within her own spirit: 'It was in December,' she says 'that my sister went forward to an altar call. Through a word of knowledge she was told that she was healed. I could not believe that and insisted that my sister continue her steroid treatment.'

It was not until 1972, however, that Dr Edwards was really convinced that healing had actually and unmistakeably occurred and this led her into a living relationship with Jesus Christ as her Lord and Saviour.

Of the remaining two channels through which God ministers healing the laying on of hands is perhaps the one which causes more comment and controversy (Mark 16:18). In this act the hands of man are related to the hands of God. It is very significant that though God has no body at all, he is spoken of in terms of many human characteristics – his feet; his legs; his hands; his arms; his shoulders; his face; his eyes; his nose; his ears; etc. Some have felt that this is the result of some kind of primitive anthropomorphism – that *God* is like *man*. The reverse in fact is taught in the Bible – that *man* is like *God*! So in the 'laying on of hands' we have a dynamic way by which power will be imparted by God to those who are being touched. When Jacob blessed his sons by placing his hands on them – it was the expression of God setting them apart for his purposes. When the Levites were being set apart as priests to God by the laying on of hands it was not simply a formal acknowledgement of their authority, but the assurance that God would protect and equip them for their ministry. In Jesus, of course, we have a unique expression of the hands of God and the hands of man coming together in unhindered perfection. There would be no difficulty for most of us if Jesus were still among us in incarnation in believing that God's hands were upon us when he laid his hands upon us. In the New Testament, consequently, those filled with the Holy Spirit (the Spirit of Jesus) believed that as they ministered in the name of Jesus (i.e. as if Jesus himself were ministering) that their hands were to those to whom they ministered as the hands of Jesus and therefore as the hands of God. It was an amazing act of faith on the part of the early Church – indeed it was what they did with their hands rather than what they did with their head and so their mouths that made people aware that Jesus was not dead. Clearly this did not become confined to the ordinary believers (e.g. Acts 9:17–19). By the laying on of hands the love, life and power of God are communicated.

Finally, Jesus gives assurance of the inherent power of biblical fellowship in Matthew 18:19,20. It seems that there are no limits to what God can do when he has a fellowship which is pure and in harmony. When Jesus prayed that last prayer to his Father, as the day dawned for his crucifixion, it was a prayer not only for himself that he might be glorified, but also for his disciples that they might be sanctified, and for us that we might be unified (John 17). The reason he gives to his Father for asking that we might be unified is 'that the world may believe that you have sent me' (John 17:20–6). Fellowship is necessary, not so much to do *us* good, but to do *him* good, and to let the *world* know that he is who he claimed to be.

So the Sleeping Giant stirs and the world becomes aware that:

We serve a living Saviour, He's in the world today:
We know that He is living, whatever men may say. . .

HALLELUJAH